CW00547872

THE FUTURE OF FINANCE

THE
FUTURE
OF
FINANCE

The Rising Tide of Fintech Lending
and the Platform Economy

FRANCESCO FILIA AND
DANIELE GUERINI

First published in Great Britain in 2024 by
Francesco Filia and Daniele Guerini,
in partnership with whitefox publishing

www.wearewhitefox.com

Copyright © Francesco Filia and Daniele Guerini, 2024

ISBN 978-1-915635-81-5
Also available as an eBook
ISBN 978-1-915635-82-2

Designed and typeset by Couper Street Type Co.
Cover design by Tomás Almeida
Project management by whitefox
Printed and bound by CPI Group (UK) Ltd, Croydon CRO 4YY

Contents

Introduction

Sometimes with the passage of time it's hard to appreciate just how much has changed. This is certainly true in relation to money, specifically banking, how we do business and how we manage our financial affairs.

Imagine for a moment that you have a time machine. Let's go back to see how business was conducted in the 1970s. You plug in the coordinates and arrive inside a shoe store in London, 1975. Owen's Shoes is a family business that has been selling shoes from the same premises on the high street for over a century. The current owner, Robert Owen, took over the business from his founder father and he grew up immersed in retail. As a boy he would work weekends, and conversation around the dinner table was always related to shoes.

To attract customers, Robert puts an advert in the Yellow Pages every year, but most of his business is passing traffic or customers deliberately travelling to the store from nearby towns, because 'Owen's' has a good reputation for selling a wide range of high-quality shoes. He does a roaring trade at the start of each new school term as parents flock to the store for hard-wearing, comfortable school shoes.

As you watch from the sidelines, you notice that most of the customers pay with cash or by cheque but some opt to use their Barclaycard. Barclaycard, introduced in 1966, was the UK's first credit card. It was handy for consumers who could opt to pay off their purchases over time but it was an administrative headache for retailers.

Like his fellow business owners, Robert has to have a manual imprint machine, commonly known as a 'zip-zap' machine. Each one comes with a box of carbon paper slips. You notice a customer pull out their credit card to pay and move a little closer to the till so you can see what's happening. Robert pulls his imprint machine from under the counter and places the customer's card on the machine, laying the carbon paper slip over the top. He then slides the handle of the machine across the card, creating an imprint of the card details, name, number and expiry date onto the slip. Robert then completes the rest of the details, including the date and amount of the transaction and the customer signs the slip to authorise the transaction. Robert tears off the top copy to give to the customer along with their receipt and keeps the second copy for his own records. The customer leaves the store with their shoes and Robert puts the slip in the till along with all the others he's taken that day.

At the end of the day, or maybe even the week, Robert collects all the carbon slips and submits them to the credit card issuer for processing. The issuer then manually processes the slips, verifies the transactions and credits Robert's bank account with the authorised amount.

This process can take anywhere from several days to a week or so.

Because of the time gap between the sale and being paid, Robert prefers cash. Some other retailers he knows on the high street have started to call an authorisation centre to get immediate approval for the transaction, but it's never immediate. Often the retailer is on hold for ten or even twenty minutes and the customer just becomes frustrated with the delay. Robert has chosen to stick with the zip-zap machine because it's more convenient for the customer and he's not selling big-ticket items.

Of course, some customers still prefer to pay by cheque and those need to be collected at the end of the day and deposited at the local branch of Robert's bank. This involves him completing a deposit slip and standing in a queue. He could put the cheques and deposit slip into a deposit envelope and drop the envelope into the secure box in the bank but he has no control over when that box will be emptied so prefers to wait in the queue, knowing that the cheques will be processed the next day. Even then, it usually takes five working days for the money to be credited into his account, sometimes longer if there is an issue with the cheque.

At the time of your visit from the future, Robert has a meeting set up with the bank manager, Tom, so he's happy to stand in the queue before the meeting. The next-door premises are up for sale and he is applying for a loan so he can purchase the building and expand the business and diversify into other products, such as handbags and luggage. He's completed a detailed loan application and now needs to present his business case to Tom. But he's feeling optimistic: the numbers make sense and he's known Tom all his life; he's part of the community and currently coaches his daughter Libby's football team but this is certainly not a social call. The good news is that he is going to be able to use his initial premises as collateral to secure the loan and he has a personal guarantor lined up if that's also needed. The meeting goes well and Tom agrees to the loan.

It's been an interesting day looking at the past, but you wonder what it might be like to visit in 2013, five years after the Global Financial Crisis (GFC). You punch the new date coordinates into your time machine and are back in the shoe store in 2013. Robert's daughter Libby is now running the business.

Libby still has a physical store but she's sold the premises that her dad bought next door. The rents are going up on the high street and footfall is dropping. Her plan is to use the money from the sale to buy a bigger out-of-town warehouse and ramp up her online presence, which has been showing real promise. But she needs a loan to cover the cost of the new premises and to upgrade her website with full ecommerce functionality.

Libby is concerned. Her dad was able to speak to Tom, the local bank manager, but those days are long gone. There is no longer a local branch of her bank in her local town and no bank manager to speak to. Instead, a helpline offers greater convenience and access. Unfortunately, she needs to sit on hold for forty minutes, only to get through to someone in Bangalore who doesn't know or care that there has been an Owen's Shoes shop in her area for 143 years. She is directed online to complete a digital form and apply for the loan she needs. She is no longer able to make a case to a person who knows the history of the business and understands that business's role in the real economy of the local area. Like every other consumer and small and medium business owner, she is at the mercy of credit scores that will determine the viability of her future based on a bunch of algorithms.

Legislation in the UK, Europe and the US has made it illegal to discriminate against people seeking funding based on religion, ethnicity, gender, marital status or age. As a woman in business, this may sound like progress for Libby. Bank managers, like everyone else on the planet, are prone to natural bias and credit scores would nullify that bias – at least in theory. Natural bias is where we tend to favour certain people over others because they are 'like us'. Bank managers, almost always middle-aged white men, were therefore much more likely to approve loans for other middle-aged white men. Credit scores were seen as the antidote whereby an unbiased computer would create scores based on other factors such as payment history, amount owed, length of credit history and credit mix. Collectively this credit score would indicate whether the person was creditworthy or not.

Libby's business is still solid in 2013, but banks have retreated from their traditional role on the high street, operating within the community. To be fair, banks had been retreating for a while, but the GFC accelerated the trend and made life harder for business owners like Libby.

Following the GFC, Central Banks applied a new approach to commercial banking to temper public outrage and ensure the crisis never happened again. More emphasis was placed on risk and on the concept of 'risk weighted assets' (RWA). Clearly, not all assets on a bank's balance sheet carry the same level of risk: some, like Treasury Notes, carry virtually no risk; others, like loans to small real estate developers are considered very risky. Changes to capital adequacy rules meant that a certain amount of capital had to be set aside based on RWA. This change prioritised loans that carried less risk. As a result, lending to SME (small- and medium-sized enterprises) business owners like Libby fell off a cliff because those clients almost always carried higher risk weightings and therefore absorbed too much of the bank's capital. The introduction and subsequent tightening of these rules effectively allowed Central Banks to more closely influence the actions of commercial banks. Consequently, high-street banks behaved more like enforcers of Central

Banks' policies and less like the drivers of economic growth and development in the real economy they used to be.

By 2013, this new approach was having a dramatic effect on huge swaths of the population, leaving too many people either unbanked or underbanked. Commercial banks had effectively pulled up the drawbridge on their traditional banking activities, including lending to consumers and SME operators like Libby.

And yet, Libby still needs money to realise her online ambitions and potentially pivot the business away from bricks and mortar entirely. Her advertising is much more sophisticated than in her dad's day when Yellow Pages and passing traffic was enough to make the business profitable. No one uses Yellow Pages anymore, or if they do they check the online version. She still puts a few adverts in the local paper around key selling times, such as the new school term and Christmas, but most of her advertising is now done on social media platforms, including Instagram and Facebook, so she can reach a wider audience who want their shoes delivered.

In her store, most of her customers pay by cash or via their credit or debit card using chip and pin technology. Libby can't remember the last time she even saw a cheque, never mind cashed one. Although the money is in her account far faster than when her dad was using zip-zap machines and depositing cheques at the local branch, reaching customers is getting harder. And, since the GFC, customers seem to have less money to spend or they are certainly less willing to spend it on shoes.

Now let's fast forward to 2030 . . .

Again, you revisit Owen's, only this time you meet James, Libby's son. You see James wake up in the morning – it's a beautiful, sunny day. After breakfast, James jumps in his car to head to the office. As soon as he starts the engine, the payment flow on his car insurance is activated. A set of cameras and sensors, combined with an artificial intelligence (AI) algorithm, constantly updates his safety score and adjusts his policy premium. The money is deducted from his cryptocurrency wallet in real time and he pays his car insurance by the second. When the car stops, he stops paying.

On the way to work, James stops by his favourite coffee shop to order breakfast and he scans his palm to execute the payment. Once again, money is transferred instantaneously to the coffee shop's account – and part of that payment flows automatically to the coffee shop's lender. Luca, the coffee shop owner, is using a financial product called a merchant cash advance (MCA). He obtained a working capital loan that is repaid through a percentage of all the future revenues processed through the palm reader he has installed. When business is good, he's able to repay the loan faster, but when revenues slow down, he's not pushed into financial distress because repayments are also slowing down.

James reaches his office. Today Owen's is a successful ecommerce business, which has branched out into selling entire outfits – including shoes! The competition from personal shopping sites and Amazon continues to be strong, but James now has many more tools that allow him to level the playing field.

On the financial side, James works with a digital bank specialised in servicing ecommerce clients. In addition to payment and foreign exchange services – making exporting easier, faster and cheaper – he has access to their lending marketplace. Here, through application programming interfaces (APIs), he is connected to a variety of specialised ecommerce lenders. Through 'Open Banking', lenders can see Owen's sales performance and advertising efficiency in real time. As a result, they can see James's cash flow, while a connection to Owen's accounting system allows them to predict when he will need money and make capital budgeting suggestions. Incredibly, some of the lenders are James's own clients!

James also has an inventory-based lending facility to finance stock purchases, and with the click of a button he can cash in on the credit he has earned on the Amazon marketplace way before it is paid out. James no longer banks with a traditional high-street bank not just because there are so few left but because the alternatives are so much better and their products are tailored to his needs. He is stunned when his mum talks about how antiquated it was back when his grandfather ran Owen's Shoes. When James's children were young, they loved playing with Papa's old zip-zap machine and playing 'shop'. How was anyone supposed to run a business like that?

At work, bureaucracy and repetitive daily activities are reduced to a minimum through the smart use of AI, automation and apps on James's phone. When Libby was running the company, sales figures were downloaded on a spreadsheet and she had to manually filter the numbers to produce insights on what was selling well and what wasn't. Today, James's spreadsheet has embedded AI capabilities. He can type, in plain English, a question he would like to be answered and the system does the job. Not only is James able to identify bestsellers, he is also provided with details on products that are often sold together, expected future sales and suggestions on the quantity of each product he should order from his suppliers. AI even factors in meteorological analysis when calculating how many umbrellas or welly boots to order. James has most of Owen's ordinary activities wrapped up using a suite of interconnected apps at his fingertips 24/7.

After James goes home at the end of the day, and before going to bed, he checks his wealth management app. The Picasso he owns through fractional ownership just sold at auction for an extraordinary premium on his purchase price. Its unique digital copy is now also featured in one of the most popular metaverse environments: Decentraland. Further, the AI robo-advisor on James's phone has already proposed a list of alternative investments, based on his risk profile, to reinvest the proceeds from the auction. Investment alternatives are not only displayed but their implementation made easy by a pure mobile user interface.

Collectively, these capabilities don't just give James more time to imagine new ways to grow the business strategically rather than getting bogged down in operational detail, they give him more freedom. More freedom to pursue other interests and spend quality time with his young family. A normal day in James's life would have been unthinkable just fifteen years earlier . . .

And yet this freedom has been predicted for a long time.

In 1848, English philosopher and political economist, John Stuart Mill, predicted that once the work of economic growth was done, a 'stationary' economy would emerge, in which we could focus on human improvement.

There would be as much scope as ever for all kinds of mental culture, and moral and social progress . . . for improving the art of living and much more likelihood of it being improved, *when minds cease to be engrossed by the art of getting on*[*]. In other words, when we are no longer consumed by making a living and can utilise technology to replace the drudgery of daily tasks, we could be liberated to design a life.

In 1930, in an essay called 'Economic Possibilities for our Grandchildren', philosopher and economist John Maynard Keynes predicted that following a *temporary phase of maladjustment due to technological unemployment* [something we are experiencing again now], *for the first time since his creation man will be faced with his real, his permanent problem – how to use his freedom from pressing economic cares, how to occupy the leisure, which science and compound interest will have won for him, to live wisely and agreeably as well*[†].

That reality is just a few short years away.

Technology is no longer a sector; it's an asset class that permeates across the full business spectrum. Every company is equipped with different degrees of technology. Traditional 'off the grid' businesses have, for the most part, been relegated to being marginal accessories of the global economy. Digital technology is a way for any business – including SMEs, the backbone of the real economy – to sweat their assets and achieve more with less: less time, less effort, less capital, less friction. Fintech is already changing the nature of business and what's possible. And it will continue to do so, not only making the whole financial system more resilient against

---

[*] Mill, J.S., *Principles of Political Economy* (John W. Parker, London, 1848).

[†] Keynes, J.M., 'Economic Possibilities for our Grandchildren', *Essays in Persuasion* (1930), https://assets.aspeninstitute.org/content/uploads/files/content/upload/Intro_and_Section_I.pdf

financial shocks like the GFC but also levelling the playing field and affording SMEs new and exciting opportunities for greater efficiency and growth that positively impacts the real economy.

> Digital technology is a way for any business, including SMEs - the backbone of the real economy - to sweat their assets and achieve more with less.

In Chapter 1, we'll take a closer look at how finance has changed over the last fifty years and how those changes have facilitated a toxic disconnect between the real economy and the financial markets, paying particular attention to the GFC of 2007/08. They say, necessity is the mother of invention. Fintech is that invention and the fallout from the GFC created the necessity. If you are already familiar with this story then feel free to jump ahead to Chapter 2, which explores the driving forces that have made fintech flourish. Chapter 3 explains the concept of embedded finance, whose purpose is to enable businesses to manage and sell innovative financial services, seamlessly integrating creative forms of payment, debit, credit, insurance and even investment into their end user experience. Chapter 4 takes a deep dive into digital lending, exploring the building blocks and resulting trends and Chapter 5 does the same for digital assets. Chapter 6 looks ahead at the opportunities and challenges so we can be ready for the future. And finally, the conclusion offers an overview of the financial landscape and hints to the future.

Chapter 1:

Banking at the Edge of Chaos

There are patterns everywhere.

They exist in nature in the astonishing geometric shapes we see in plants like Aloe Polyphylla or flowers like the Dahlia. Often, they appear so perfect, so organised and so intricate that they resemble works of art. We see patterns in crystals, weather systems, in the behaviour of people and habits of animals, in the murmuration of birds and even in the organisation of galaxies. And patterns are also present within complex systems such as the economy.

There are patterns in the real economy and there are patterns in financial markets.

These patterns emerge from the initial conditions and evolve over time. Global patterns in anything emerge when individuals act locally so that what we see on a big scale is a consequence of what we see on a small scale. What we see when we look at a human being (big) is a consequence of what is coded into their DNA (small). What we see in an economy is the consequence of thousands of little or larger shifts at a local level. Complex dynamic systems behave non-linearly, through amplifying dynamics and into runaway effects. Amplifying dynamics refer to positive feedback loops that lead to the magnification of certain factors within a system, which can, in turn, lead to exponential growth (runaway effects) or reinforcement of specific behaviours. The systems themselves can appear orchestrated, but there is no architect or conductor, just systems following rules laid down through evolution.

And the analysis of critical transitions in complex adaptive systems helps to shed light on disruptions in both nature and financial markets – the radical changes that happen at tipping points when critical thresholds are passed. Systems theory teaches us that the system is always larger and more relevant than the sum of its parts. It takes on a life of its own. And there are always system interdependencies and interplays, so-called positive and negative 'feedback loops'. These loops are essential concepts that describe how a system responds to changes or disturbances. Whereas positive feedback loops amplify or reinforce the initial change or disturbance, leading to a self-reinforcing cycle that pushes away from the original state, a negative feedback loop counteracts or dampens the effect of the initial change or disturbance helping to stabilise the system and bring it back toward its original state.

After an external shock to the financial system, like the GFC or Covid pandemic, positive feedback loops send a system into transition (runaway effect) and into a new stable state.

In the case of banking post-GFC, positive feedback loops moved the system away from the traditional commercial banking approach and favoured the development of the Platform Economy whereas, after a similar external shock, negative feedback loops act as system stabilisers that make the system return to its original state, in this case a market economy centred on commercial banks alone. Clearly, in the case of the GFC shock, positive feedback loops had a dominating effect over negative feedback loops.

We can see these system interdependencies and interplays in action in the financial system. For a very long time there was a logical and tangible relationship between the financial markets and the real economy (Figure 1.1).

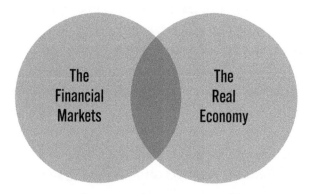

Figure 1.1: The Connection Between the Financial Markets and the Real Economy in the Past

This made sense, even to those unfamiliar with the unwritten rules that created those systems in the first place. At a very fundamental level, the role of financial markets and capital markets is essentially a mechanism of efficient allocation of capital to the real economy, to the worthy projects waiting in line to be funded and supported.

When there was growth in the real economy, it was usually accompanied by high employment, with products and services being made and sold profitably, which was then reflected in a country's gross domestic product (GDP). And the financial market reflected that prosperity. Plenty of capital was made available to thriving individuals and companies and equity markets increased in value over an extended period.

Conversely, if the real economy slowed down, there was

usually a corresponding increase in unemployment and decrease in demand for products and services. This contraction in the real economy was reflected in the financial market, which would also usually drop in value. And as a result, the markets became more risk averse and often reduced the amount of capital available for investments and consumption, thus exacerbating the economic slowdown. Whatever happened in the real economy influenced the financial market and vice versa – and yet that is no longer true.

Since the GFC of 2008, the connection between financial markets and the real economy has been mediated and disrupted by external factors, the most evident of which is the increased role of Central Banks. Regrettably, the unintended and far-reaching consequence has been to impair efficient allocation of resources to the real economy. The result is two separate, disconnected realities (Figure 1.2).

Since the GFC, the connection between financial markets and the real economy has been mediated and disrupted by external factors, the most evident of which is the increased role of Central Banks.

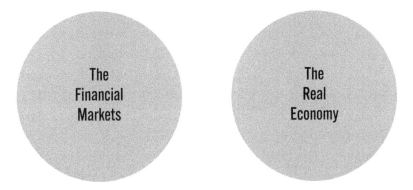

Figure 1.2: The Emerging Disconnect Between the Financial Markets and the Real Economy

This disconnect is not academic or theoretical – it is having a measurable impact on real people living real lives, starting, running and growing real businesses. It is therefore important to understand the changes that occurred at a local level that contributed to this seismic change in global patterns. The change, subtle at first, has reverberated throughout the entire financial system and taken on a life of its own, affecting leverage levels, borrowers' behaviour, implied volatility, market structure and the shape of the capital markets over the long term.

This disconnect did not happen overnight and, in all fairness, it is not just simply the consequence of the changing role of Central Banks. It is the consequence of a long series of seemingly small changes that took place over decades.

The Path to Disruption

Financial market is a broad term that refers to a marketplace where buyers and sellers participate in the trade of financial assets such as stocks, bonds, currencies, commodities and derivatives. These markets facilitate the flow of capital between investors, borrowers and savers.

If, as an example, we look at stocks, we can see a distinct shift in the patterns that influence share prices. If we were to utilise our time machine again and travel back to the 1950s, we would see that the CEOs of publicly listed companies, those companies that make up the stock market, were paid a salary that was, at most, twenty times what the average employee in that company earned.

This established pattern of senior executive remuneration started to change in 1970, at least in theory, when economist Milton Friedman wrote an article in the *New York Times* stating that the sole purpose of business was to make money for its shareholders. Friedman suggested that any business executive who pursued a goal other than making money for shareholders was *an unwitting puppet of the intellectual forces that have been undermining the basis of a free society these past decades*, going so far as to accuse such leaders of becoming, *unelected government officials* who were illegally taxing employers and customers. Although this was considered a highly controversial opinion at a time when CEOs and C-suite leaders were viewed as stewards and their role was to work for the good of all stakeholders, not just shareholders, Friedman didn't include an action plan.

Six years later, that changed when finance Professor Michael Jensen and William Meckling of the Simon School of Business at the University of Rochester published a paper that would trigger a pattern shift toward shareholder value maximisation.

Despite offering no evidence, Jensen and Meckling suggested that shareholders were being duped out of higher returns because of the 'principal-agent problem', namely that the shareholder (principal) was often disadvantaged by the firm's senior executives (agents) because there was an implicit incentive for those agents to optimise their own self-interest and not necessarily the interest of the shareholders. Business class travel and nice company cars were effectively reducing shareholder returns. Their solution, put forward in their 'agency theory', was to make senior executives shareholders. Clearly, if the agents became principals, then their objectives would align and there would no longer be a principal-agent problem!

Their paper became the single most frequently cited article in business academia and it provided a way to turn

Friedman's earlier vision into a commercial reality. When Friedman suggested maximising shareholder return, although he didn't use that term, stock-based compensation packages accounted for less than one per cent of CEO remuneration. Following Jensen and Meckling's suggestion (1976), executive compensation became increasingly stock-based. By 2009, stock-based remuneration accounted for up to 97 per cent of leadership remuneration*. Today you would now be hard pressed to find any senior executives in any publicly listed company that did not include a sizeable share-based compensation package in their incentive plan.

The unintended consequence of this shift is that senior leaders, by dint of nothing more than human nature, have become much more focused on short-term results over long-term strategic planning. It is the short-term results that contribute to their personal wealth, not long-range thinking. In other words, senior executives have a clear incentive to influence financial markets rather than the fundamentals of the businesses they run. In what is, at the very least, an ironic twist, this pattern shift from long-term stewardship for the betterment of all the stakeholders to short-term shareholder value maximisation has created the very problem that Jensen and Meckling sought to prevent. Before the inclusion of share options in senior executive remuneration packages there was no or little evidence of the principal-agent problem being a real-world problem beyond an occasional anecdote. Since, however, there is a mountain of evidence of everything from salaries untethered to reality, corporate 'smartest guys in the

---

* Martin, R.L., *Fixing the Game: How Runaway Expectations Broke the Economy, and How to Get Back to Reality* (Harvard Business School Press, Boston, 2011).

room'-style corruption, market manipulations, backdated options scandals and outright fraud.

This escalating short-termism also meant that the fundamentals of a business became far less important, to the point of almost being irrelevant. By making senior leaders shareholders, it inadvertently shifted the focus from the real economy to focus almost solely on the share price and predictions of expected future income in the financial market. Businesses, even publicly traded businesses, operate in the real economy. They employ people who spend their wages in their communities and they buy things, thus driving the real economy. But when the focus shifts from strategic long-term planning and how to maximise productivity and profit in the real economy to how best to control the narrative around next quarter's earnings, then the game is forever changed.

> Making senior leaders shareholders inadvertently shifted the focus from the real economy to focus almost solely on the share price and predictions of expected future income in the financial market.

Whether senior leaders receive a bumper bonus, is no longer just down to the fundamentals of the business, it's down to how that business is perceived by investors or equity analysts and how well they are expected to do in the future. Over time, the price of a stock has become the biggest driver of wealth creation for senior leaders of publicly listed companies. Needless to say, this can and does distort executive behaviour. Compensation has become increasingly linked to expectations rather than results. And it is now far easier to game the system. Promise the world, sell the future story of the business, sit back as share price inflation does the rest and leave the business before the results are in. CEOs have become more like football managers, almost guaranteed to be sacked (or to leave before they are sacked). But it doesn't really matter; they have already made huge bonuses, go on to the next position, publicly downgrade the stock price on arrival to lament the efforts of the previous CEO (a practice so common it's called 'kitchen sinking') only to rinse and repeat. In the 1950s the difference between CEO pay and the average worker was 20:1, then came the celebrity CEOs and shareholder maximisation and that ratio skyrocketed. In the UK the average CEO pay is 118 times greater than the average worker in that firm*. In the US the average ratio is 272:1[†]. And there have been eye-watering exceptions – 1,935:1 in the UK[‡] and 1,763:1 in the US[§].

It's worth pointing out that executives are incentivised to be overly optimistic about the future, not just because their future pay depends on it but because that's what's now demanded of them by their shareholders and the Board.

Income inequality is one problem, but corporate inequality is also stifling innovation and real productivity and distorting economic dynamics. Central Banks inundated the market with liquidity, but, because they didn't have the technology to serve the smaller market segment efficiently, almost all that liquidity went to large companies, further exacerbating

---

* No Author, 'Executive pay rises amid cost-of-living crisis', ICAEW Insights (2023).

† Kaplan, J., 'CEOs made 272 times more than their workers in 2022, earning nearly $17 million on average', *Business Insider* (2023).

‡ CIPD, 'Executive pay in the FTSE 100: 2020 review' (2020).

§ Mosteller, A., 'CEO vs. Employee Salaries at America's Top Companies', business.org (2021).

the divide between big and small companies. SMEs were left behind, massively hindering their growth prospects and feeding the escalating divide between big and small companies in the real economy and the financial market.

The disconnect between the value of a business as measured by the fundamentals and its perception in financial markets was further fractured by high frequency trading (HFT). High frequency traders are not interested in the fundamentals of a business such as profit margins, ROI, cash flow forecasts or growth metrics. They are not concerned with debt levels, value metrics or operational efficiency. Instead, they use algorithms to predict small changes in the price of a stock over very short timeframes.

To explain HFT, we need to take a step back. Electronic trading became possible for the first time following significant deregulation in the financial industry in October 1986. Known as the 'Big Bang' this involved market deregulation, which allowed for increased competition and the removal of barriers between different financial activities. The end of fixed commissions and the integration of various financial services, including banking, securities trading and insurance (previously strictly separated), collectively allowed for the creation of much larger financial institutions. In addition, the Big Bang replaced the traditional open outcry system of trading on the floor of the London Stock Exchange and other exchanges with electronic trading systems to make trading faster and more efficient.

What emerged were investment firms that were only looking at the patterns of trading activity. Shares were therefore not bought and sold by a human being who was assessing the stability and value of a company in the way Benjamin Graham or Warren Buffet would trade. Instead, a machine was trading the shares, based on market-wide patterns or micro movements in a sector or stock. The advent of high-speed internet connectivity allowed trading over shorter and shorter time horizons, and today an HFT firm can buy and sell a stock multiple times – literally in the blink of an eye. While it is certainly very hard to measure the impact of HFT on stock prices, around 60 to 70 per cent of stock trading on the main exchanges can be classified as high frequency trading. This means that the majority of all the daily transactions in equities today are totally disconnected from fundamentals and the real economy.

> This means that the majority of all the daily transactions in equities today are totally disconnected from fundamentals and the real economy.

Meanwhile, over in the real economy, there were mixed results. Although GDP growth averaged 3.5 per cent per year in the UK between 1981 and 1989, compared with just 2.4 per cent in the 1970s, interest rates were high, starting the decade at 16 per cent*! By the late 1980s, the Lawson Boom kicked in, driven by deregulation in the financial markets, lower interest rates and increased trade. The right to buy gave ordinary people the right to buy their council house and home ownership increased dramatically, pushing up house prices. On the flip side, many manufacturing jobs were lost when companies moved overseas for lower wages. Highly paid jobs such as coal mining disappeared, devastating

---

* Official Bank Rate History, Bank of England, https://www. bankofengland.co.uk/boeapps/database/Bank-Rate.asp [accessed 13 October 2023].

communities, and unemployment hit a record high of 3 million in 1986[*].

Of course, busts usually follow booms, and the 1990s started with a severe recession largely due to a global economic downturn. A return to high interest rates coupled with a decline in consumer spending and business investment contributed to economic contraction. This situation was made worse in the UK by the withdrawal from the European Exchange Rate Mechanism (ERM) after failing to maintain the required currency exchange rate. This event, known as 'Black Wednesday', led to a sharp devaluation of the British Pound and had significant economic consequences in the real economy – especially for those businesses that were importing and exporting. In 1995, the collapse of the UK's oldest merchant bank, Barings, raised questions about the stability of financial institutions and the fragility of the system they operated in but these fears were swept under the carpet and the collapse was blamed on a single 'rogue trader', Nick Leeson.

The 1990s saw a rise in the use of credit cards and a steep growth in consumer debt, a tool used in the real economy to soften the edges of a turbulent economy. Although a new boom emerged in the late 1990s due to technology, this was the run-up to the dot.com crash of 2000–2001.

Across the Atlantic, the 1980s and 90s were a mixed bag too. During the 1980s President Ronald Reagan, Margaret Thatcher's ideological soul mate, pursued similar policies, including breaking the unions and significant financial

---

[*] Choksi, K., 'How the UK's Economic Boom in the 1980s Changed the Country Forever', Path Intelligence (2022).

deregulation. Although what led to the global financial crisis was complex and multi-causal, policies enacted under Thatcher and Reagan undoubtedly laid the groundwork for the crisis to unfold. In the US, for example, their 'Big Bang' was the repeal, in 1999, of parts of the Glass-Steagall legislation. This legislation was adopted in 1933 following the Great Depression, which was triggered by the 1929 stock market crash and was designed to make a future crash less likely. Its partial repeal in 1999 allowed financial institutions to mix their commercial, risk-averse operations with their proprietary trading or risk-taking operations*. Prior to this, banks were either a commercial bank or an investment bank. The repeal allowed them to be both, leading to the creation of financial behemoths with massive balance sheets that would later be considered 'too big to fail' (more on that in a moment).

The change incentivised banks to become bigger and reap more profit. With hindsight, it is easy to see how this incentivisation would lead to the steep increase in the aggressive sales tactics that occurred. Again, it is a result of little more than human nature. Essentially, what happened was the creation of a perfect storm fed by significant deregulation, low interest rates, badly designed incentive schemes, greed, hubris and a blind optimism that housing markets always go up.

According to the IMF, *The crisis that began as the US 'sub-prime' crisis in the summer of 2007 spread to a number of other advanced economies through a combination of direct exposures to subprime assets, the gradual loss of confidence*

---

* Maverick, J.B., 'Consequences of the Glass-Steagall Act Repeal', Investopedia (2019).

in a number of asset classes and the drying-up of whole-sale financial markets. In this process it came to expose 'home-grown' financial imbalances in a number of advanced economies, typically characterized by an overreliance on wholesale funding sources by the banking system and asset bubbles in residential property markets*.

In short, lending became untethered from reality – again, another indicator of the big disconnect between the real economy and the financial markets. The central issue that tipped the global system into chaos was mortgage lending. Pre-deregulation, if someone wanted a mortgage to buy a home, they would need to prove that they were a 'prime' borrower. This entailed, amongst other things, having saved a deposit, usually 20 per cent of the value of the property, and providing evidence that their income was sufficient to cover the mortgage repayments. Most banks would only lend three times the potential borrower's salary. If you ticked those and a few other boxes, the loan was approved. If not, it was rejected.

To boost profits, however, banks started to lend vast sums of money to 'subprime' borrowers in a low document or no document lending spree. Subprime customers were people who didn't have any deposit and didn't necessarily have the income to repay the mortgage. The assumption was that the housing market was booming, so even if the borrower defaulted on the loan, the underlying asset, the home's value, would be sufficient to cover any loss. This meant that people were buying homes they could not afford.

---

*   Merrouche, O. and Nier, E., 'What Caused the Global Financial Crisis?', *Evidence on the Drivers of Financial Imbalances 1999–2007*, IMF Working Paper (2010).

In many instances banks such as the Northern Rock Building Society in the UK or Countrywide Financial and the IndyMac Bank in the US, were offering 110 per cent mortgages – meaning, not only did the borrower not need to demonstrate financial prudence to save a deposit, they could buy a home for $300,000 and get a nice $30,000 bonus payment! It was insane. And it was the euphoria of financial markets that allowed this insanity to thrive, regardless of what common sense and real economy indicators were suggesting.

When someone borrows money, the cost is made up of the 'base rate' or rate at which the Central Bank offers money to financial institutions plus a 'risk premium'. This risk premium, in the form of additional interest, grows as a function of risk or perceived risk. During this time, between 2005 and 2006, the premium required to borrow for risky assets reached record low levels creating a very fertile ground for the proliferation of Collateralized Loan Obligations (CLOs). CLOs contained a pool of loans, in this case mortgages, that were bundled together and sold to investors on the secondary market – fund managers or institutional investors. The idea being that the investor then benefits from the cash flows from the interest and principal payments made by the borrowers of the underlying loans.

But what happens to those cash flows when those borrowers are not paying their loans or they simply send their keys back to the lender in the mail, a practice known as 'jingle mail'? To make matters worse, these CLOs were astonishingly complex. They were sliced into bonds depending on the priority of payments from the cash flow of the underlying mortgages. And these CLOs included both prime and subprime loans. This is like baking an apple pie and adding a little rotten apple in the hope that the good apples will mask the taste of the bad apples. Of course, it rarely works and the whole pie is ruined. Although it was the job of rating agencies, such as Standard & Poor's, Moody's and Fitch, to assess how much rotten apple was in each product and assign risk ratings to CLO bonds, their complexity made it difficult. Furthermore, rating agencies were also paid handsomely to provide credit ratings to CLOs by those very banks that were trying to place them in the market. Disappointing credit ratings could risk jeopardising the commercial relationship and this inherent conflict of interest played a major role in the development of the GFC, as the US government's Financial Crisis Enquiry later recognized[*].

When the housing bubble inevitably burst, it came to light that these agencies and others had allocated AAA ratings (minimal risk) to investments that were a lot riskier than expected because they were stuffed with bad subprime loans.

Although commentators often say that no one saw the crash coming, there *were* signs. In May 2006, J.P. Morgan warned clients of a housing downturn. In August the same year, the yield curve inverted, signalling that a recession was likely within a year or so. The yield curve is a graphical representation of interest rates on deposits for a range of maturities and provides insights into market expectations and the overall health of the economy. In November 2006, UBS sounded the alarm about an impending crisis in the US housing market.

In April 2007, New Century, an American real estate investment trust specialising in subprime lending, filed for bankruptcy. In June, Bear Stears bailed out two of its hedge

---

[*] *The Financial Crisis Inquiry Report*, US Government (2011).

funds with a $20 billion exposure to CDOs but assured the market that the problem was contained. The funds were liquidated a month later. In August 2007, American Home Mortgage filed for bankruptcy and, on the 9th of that month, BNP Paribas, France's largest bank, announced it was freezing three of its funds. Their reason? *The complete evaporation of liquidity in certain market segments of the US securitisation market has made it impossible to value certain assets fairly regardless of their quality or credit rating.*[*]

Fast forward through more warnings, a bank run, more bankruptcies, a few bailouts and an economic stimulus package and we reach the climax of the subprime mortgage crisis: the collapse of Lehman Brothers on 15th September 2008. After being notified of a pending credit downgrade due to Lehman's heavy position in subprime mortgages, the Federal Reserve summoned several banks to try to find a solution. But discussions failed and Lehman became the biggest bankruptcy in US history, involving more than $600 billion in assets.

The collapse of Lehman triggered a massive drop in the markets and created a chain reaction that brought the global financial system to its knees. And the abiding lesson taken from the chaos by Central Banks everywhere was that some banks were just 'too big to fail'. In other words, the damage done to the entire financial system because of the Lehman collapse was so severe that it should never be allowed to happen again.

Central Banks in various jurisdictions recognised the serious and profound 'contagion risk' associated with such

---

[*] Tooze, A., *Crashed: How a Decade of Financial Crises Changed the World* (Penguin, London, 2018).

a huge collapse and chose to ensure it would never happen again by stepping in via bank bailouts. This move, whilst understandable, effectively allowed for the privatisation of the profits and socialisation of all the losses. In other words, the banks could partake in highly risky behaviour to create astonishing profits but, when that risky behaviour led to serious losses, a safety net was provided to cushion the financial blow. All upside. No downside.

The ensuing chaos in the banking sector had a profound impact in financial markets, and on the real economy. People were angry, and rightly so, and trust in financial institutions reached rock bottom. We will come back to this in the following chapters, but it was no coincidence that the first ever Bitcoin was mined in January 2009. Embedded in the genesis block of the Bitcoin blockchain is the text: *The Times Jan/03/2009 Chancellor on brink of second bailout for banks.* As well as timestamping the genesis block of Bitcoin, the reference to further bank bailouts is widely recognised as a deliberate swipe at the instability of the global financial system laid bare by the GFC*.

Real lives were destroyed by the crash. And the anger was certainly felt by real people in the real economy and those people vote. A lot of political pressure was exerted on governments, and governments in turn applied pressure on Central Banks. Central Banks in turn applied pressure on commercial banks, turning them into dependent entities charged with enforcing new regulatory requirements rather than community-based supporters of real business owners

---

* Cooke, G.C., *Web3: The End of Business as Usual* (Whitefox, London, 2023).

driving the real economy. It certainly wasn't a vote-winning strategy to use taxpayers' money, money raised by work conducted in the real economy, to bail out the banking sector's greed and hubris.

Voters demanded action and governments around the world insisted on renewed regulation to dampen the anger of their voting public. For example, the Basel Accords, published in 1988 and enforced by the G10 in 1992, were updated. Basel I created a framework for market risk. Basel II, published in 2004, introduced 'three pillars' to create a new capital framework to supersede Basel I. Those pillars were:

1. Minimum capital requirements, which sought to develop and expand the standardised rules set out in the 1988 Accord;
2. Supervisory review of an institution's capital adequacy and internal assessment process;
3. Effective use of disclosure as a lever to strengthen market discipline and encourage sound banking practices.

Clearly, 'encouraging' sound banking practices was not enough. Basel III reforms, published in 2010/11 in response to the GFC, introduced stricter controls, including:

- Higher minimum capital requirements;
- Additional capital buffers to provide extra protection in challenging times;
- Liquidity coverage measures to guarantee the ability to cover shor-term liquidity needs;
- Maximum leverage ratios, to limit the build-up of leverage, irrespective of asset risk weightings.

This time around, measures were a lot more tangible. However, even though Basel III was intended as a set of reform measures to improve regulation, supervision and risk management in the international banking sector, it has created some unintended consequences that have impacted the real economy in profoundly negative ways.

Lending to SMEs by financial institutions has steadily declined over the past decade because of the risk weighting on such loans and, almost ten years on, the process is still ongoing. For example, a report by Oxera commissioned by SME lender Allica in 2023, found that changes to UK bank capital rules proposed by the Prudential Regulatory Authority (PRA) of the UK could result in a further £44 billion drop in lending to SMEs, approximating a 20 per cent decline.

Lending to SMEs by financial institutions has steadily declined over the past decade.

Not only that, PRA's proposed 100 per cent minimum risk weight floor for SME business loans secured on property (substantially higher than international standards) would mean unsecured SME loans would have lower risk weights than certain secured loans, potentially incentivising banks to favour riskier lending[*], the exact opposite of what was intended by Basel III.

And this is a major issue for the real economy.

It is SMEs, not large corporates, that make up the backbone of the real economy. According to the World Bank, SMEs make

---

[*] No Author, 'Change to bank capital rules could result in £44bn drop in SME lending', Credit Connect (2023).

up more than 90 per cent of businesses and employ around two-thirds of the workforce in most economies (Figure 1.3).

Country	SME %	Employment %	GDP %
Austria (2015)	99.7%	67.5%	
Brazil (2018)	98.5%	41.0%	27.0%
Canada (2016)	98.0%	70.1%	
Czech Republic (2016)	99.8%	58.4%	
Estonia (2015)	90.7%	79.6%	76.5%
Finland (2015)	99.3%	59.4%	
Japan (2014)	99.7%	70.1%	
Luxembourg (2014)	99.5%	68.5%	68.7%
Portugal (2015)	99.7%	78.8%	
Serbia (2015)	99.8%	65.0%	58.0%
Sweden (2018)	99.0%	60.0%	47.0%
Thailand (2015)	99.7%	80.4%	41.1%
United Kingdom (2022)	99.9%	61.0%	51.0%
United States (2021)	99.9%	60.0%	44.0%

Figure 1.3: Critical Role of SMEs in the Real Economy

The International Finance Corporation suggests it's even worse when you look at the micro, small and medium enterprise (MSME) sector. Their MSME Gap Assessment Report said that 65 million firms, or 40 per cent of MSMEs in developing countries, have an unmet global financing need of $5.2 TRILLION every year. A further $2 trillion exists in the developed world, meaning there is currently an unmet global financial need of around $7 trillion. These are staggering numbers.

In Europe, bank financing is currently the most important external source of funding for small to medium-sized enterprises (SMEs) making up around 70 per cent of external financing. This dependence has arisen historically and has also been supported by the ECB's monetary policies on credit availability since the crisis of 2007, but the implementation of Basel III and the future implementation of Basel IV will undoubtedly increase funding costs. These changes will make banks even less willing to extend loans, particularly to SMEs with below-average creditworthiness. Allianz estimate that funding costs may increase by more than 100 basis points for companies with low credit quality[*].

Although well intentioned and much needed, it is feared that Basel III's approach to risk, which is based on risk weights derived from the past, is failing to account for the uncertainty of the future and the opportunities provided by technological advancement. An OECD study suggested that: *Capital regulation based on risk-weighted assets encourages innovation designed to circumvent regulatory requirements and shifts banks' focus away from their core economic functions.* It adds: *Tighter capital requirements based on risk-weighted assets aim to increase the loss-absorption capacity of the banking system, but also increase the incentives of banks to bypass the regulatory framework. New liquidity regulation, notwithstanding its good intentions, is another likely candidate to increase bank incentives to exploit regulation[†].*

Unfortunately, Basel III offers a backward-looking solution to risk assessment. The GFC was the biggest financial shock of the century and, consequently, the avoidance of a similar situation in the future represented the main objective of Basel confrontations ever since. The message was clear: something went wrong, we analysed what went wrong and

---

[*] No Author, 'European regulatory changes will make banks less willing to lend to SMEs', Allianz Trade (2019).

[†] Slovik, P., 'Systemically Important Banks and Capital Regulation Challenges', *OECD Economics Department Working Papers*, No. 916 (OECD Publishing, Paris, 2012).

we propose changes to minimise the probability of the same thing happening again. While logical, this approach fails to consider that financial systems are complex, interconnected and constantly changing systems and that, while it is extremely important to learn from the past, it is equally important to look to the future.

For example, the introduction of real-time data analysis in risk underwriting could represent a major positive change for the financial industry. Technology is already allowing SMEs to easily share more and more real-time data with their financial service providers. Open Banking provides live access to a company's cash flow as it is generated and the use of third-party technology creates additional sets of data that could provide a more accurate financial view of a business than ever before. Ecommerce merchants can be judged based on the metrics in their Shopify, Amazon or Google Ads accounts to an extent that was unimaginable fifteen years ago. Freelancers' ability to repay a loan can be influenced by the analysis of their accounts on the freelancer platforms they use. If we look at 'traditional finance', the hedge fund industry was the first to pioneer this philosophy. Unlike a bank during a risk underwriting process, hedge funds clearly can't force companies to share their real-time data. However, they developed proxies to assess the health of a business using a variety of ingenious sources. Examples include the use of credit card data to assess changes in the market share of consumer goods companies or satellites to track the flow of goods in and out of factories[*].

---

[*] 'Alternative Data (Finance)', Wikipedia, https://en.wikipedia.org/wiki/Alternative_data_(finance) [accessed 20 November 2023].

New fintech companies are taking full advantage of these new data sources and are using them in their risk underwriting practices on a regular basis. They gather as much real-time information as possible and create brand new datasets from the behaviour of their clients. For example, the way you fill in an online form may influence the possibility of a loan application being rejected. A framework to structurally direct the whole financial services industry to move in that direction would certainly improve risk assessment globally. Data is the new weapon that will determine the winner in the battle for the future of finance.

Data is the new weapon that will determine the winner in the battle for the future of finance.

The ultimate consequence of the GFC and subsequent reaction of the Central Banks is simple. SMEs are increasingly unbanked or underbanked and this is having a knock-on effect in the real economy. It is not financial markets that drive GDP, it's businesses up and down the country, employing people, making things, delivering services and buying and selling products all over the world.

Traditional, high-street banks are simply disappearing for a huge swath of the population, including consumers and SMEs. And this disappearance is not just metaphorical.

Over the past three decades, the number of local bank branches, the kind that the owners of Owen's Shoes would visit to discuss funding needs, has fallen steadily. According to the House of Commons Library there were 21,643 bank or building society branches in the UK in 1986. By 2014 there were 10,565. A loss of 51 per cent of the network or 11,078 bank or building society branches. Using ONS data, that number has since dropped even further to 8,060 branches in 2022* (Figure 1.4).

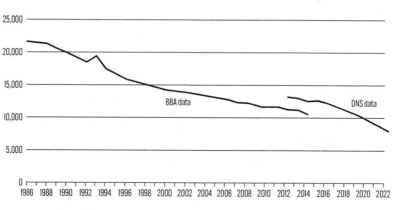

Figure 1.4: Bank and Building Society Branches in the UK
Source: UK House of Commons Library

Following another round of closures in the second half of 2023, consumer group Which? predicted there would be a little over 4,000 branches left in the UK by the end of the year. Whereas the initial wave of closures was due largely to bank consolidation after the crisis, the more recent closures come on the back of a digital revolution. There was an increased uptake in digital alternatives, supercharged by the Covid pandemic.

As Sam Richardson, deputy editor of Which? Money said, *A closed bank branch doesn't just mean one less place to withdraw or deposit cash locally, it also makes getting access to face-to-face banking services harder — something that is*

---

* Booth, L., Statistics on access to cash, bank branches and ATMs, House of Commons Library (2023).

particularly important for more vulnerable customers*. We would argue that those 'vulnerable customers' now include business owners of SMEs.

And the situation in the EU is no better.

According to the European Central Bank (ECB), structural financial indicators show a further decline in the number of bank branches in the EU, averaging 8.62 per cent across member states since 2000. This equates to the closure of over 12,000 branches and contractions were observed in 24 of the 27 countries, down by between 2.28 per cent and 30.66 per cent. The number of employees in these credit institutions also fell in the 22 EU member states, a trend that has been observed since 2008†.

Whatever the array of factors that contributed to the decimation of bank branches, the result is the same: high-street banks are gone. They have effectively left the real economy in favour of the financial market or fake economy.

And they really are fake markets.

The Central Bank bailouts taught banking that it was OK to take crazy risks because, if it all went south, they were still too big to fail and the Central Banks would, once again, step in to save the day. This unintended consequence became known as the 'Fed Put'. Banks and investors didn't really need to worry too much about the performance of the financial markets because the GFC taught them that the US Federal Reserve (and other Central Banks) would not allow the markets to fall beyond a certain threshold, around 20–25

* Venkataramakrishnan, S., 'More than one in eight UK bank branches to close in 2023', *Financial Times* (2023).

† No Author, *EU structural financial indicators: end of 2020*, European Central Bank (2021).

per cent, before issuing a rescue package involving lower interest rates and more quantitative easing (printing more money).

The fear was that a bigger drop could set off a chain reaction of bad debts that could destabilise the biggest banks and cause a crisis that would make 2008 look mild.[*] Hence the 'Fed Put', *put* being an option trading instrument that allows investors to make money when the market goes down. In this scenario the Fed is ensuring that there really isn't that much risk that the market will go down too much.

And they are using all the tools at their disposal to that effect, from cutting interest rates to record lows to buying bonds in the open market to injecting more liquidity into the system. And of course, this has inflated the financial market even more, creating an even bigger disconnect between the financial market and the real economy. Insane valuations on untested businesses are accepted as the new norm and the fundamentals of a business, under pressure for many years, have finally given way to momentum and spin. The 'Fed Put' is creating a very tangible distortion: investors are not afraid of investing in risky assets. If things improve, they will reap the benefits; if things get worse, the Fed will step in and counterbalance the negative factors, thus preventing the value of assets from falling further.

When we look at the markets of 2016 to 2022, you can see the Fed Put in action (Figure 1.5).

---

[*] Jones, E.T. and Altunbas, Y., 'Stock markets have been a one-way bet for many years thanks to the "Fed Put" – but those days are over', *The Conversation* (21 February 2022).

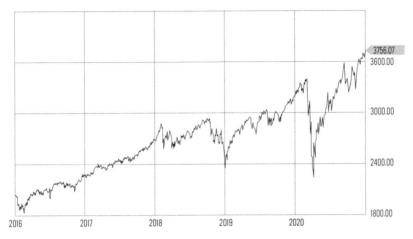

Figure 1.5: The Fed Put illustrated on the S&P 500

To put things into context, after the GFC and the 2009–2010 rebound, there has been a second period of extensive risk aversion and market weakness around 2011–2012. There were a lot of doubts about the quality of the assets on the balance sheet of US banks and fears about public finances of the weakest countries in the European Union. Concerns about the Greek, Italian, Spanish and Portuguese economies all surfaced at various times to different degrees together with questions around the whole Euro system. And then, on 26 July 2012, Mario Draghi, then President of the European Central Bank, pronounced three magic words that saved the Euro: 'whatever it takes*'. These words can be seen as the European translation of the 'Fed Put' and led to a recovery in the equity markets that lasted for years.

---

* Speech by Mario Draghi, President of the European Central Bank at the Global Investment Conference in London 26 July 2012, https://www.ecb.europa.eu/press/key/date/2012/html/sp120726. en.html [accessed 20 November 2023].

What is interesting is what happened in the medium term. Between 2016 and 2020, we experienced a series of macro headwinds that, from time to time, pushed equity markets lower, yet, every single time, the recovery was sharp and led to new highs. The most emblematic example is the March 2020 crash, at the peak of uncertainty related to the global pandemic. While the whole world went into lockdown, something that had never happened before, markets collapsed dramatically in one of the fastest falls ever. While this is a normal market reaction to external, high-impact factors, the recovery was not a normal reaction.

While airplanes remained grounded, hotels were still empty, the Olympics were cancelled and offices were deserted, markets recovered almost all their losses in just three months. Nothing had changed in the real economy, and we were still a long way from either a vaccine or normality. However, Central Banks and governments around the world had already made clear what they would be doing. That was enough. No need to panic.

Irrespective of the underlying economy, the Fed Put worked its magic once again in the fake financial markets. The magnitude and duration of these artificial flows of money from global Central Banks coupled with an explosion in passive investment vehicles managed to overwhelm and narcotise data-dependency and macro factors – things that still matter in the real economy[*]. Normally, markets respond to data from the real economy but once Central Banks started to interfere, they broke that relationship, and

---

[*] Fasanara Research Team, *The Market Economy in 2025: A Visualization Exercise* (2020).

investors' actions became detached from the reality of hard data.

Over the last ten years, we've seen a significant 'rise of the machines' in passive investment strategies. While there are still human beings assessing value based on fundamentals, there are a lot of investment vehicles simply running on autopilot, executing trades based on market patterns and algorithms. There may be different degrees of autopilot, but it's still autopilot. In addition, technological advance has put investment platforms and tools in the hands of consumers and fund managers alike, creating 'hot money'.

Hot money describes the reality that's created when technology facilitates the rapid movement of highly liquid money between and across financial markets as investors seek to take advantage of temporary market opportunities.

In days gone by, if someone wanted to invest, they would at least have to call or email their broker or financial advisor to execute the trade. The process might take a day or so, maybe longer. But those intermediaries are now disappearing, and technology and various trading platforms are giving real-time access to market – and there's always a market open somewhere in the world. There is no buffer zone that can help a company ride out bad news or poor results. Instead, investors pile out of the stock creating 'flash-crashes' when the price of a stock or several stocks take a brief but violent nose dive only to recover quickly afterwards. Is it really any wonder that CEOs and C-suite leaders spend so much time managing the narrative and keeping analysts happy when even the whiff of bad news or unexpected results can lead to a flash-crash?

The GameStop saga of 2021 is perhaps the best example of hot money in recent years. GameStop, an American chain

of bricks-and-mortar video game stores, was already ideo-
logically disconnected from the real world. Digital distribution,
where gamers were simply downloading games, together with
reduced footfall following Covid was having a negative impact
on GameStop. As a result, it attracted investors who heavily
shorted the stock. In other words, investors were betting that
the company share price was going to continue to fall.

But some influencers on the online communities of Reddit
and YouTube got involved. The Reddit forum was well
known for discussing meme stocks and high-risk stock
transactions and observers converged around the idea that, if
they all worked together, they could trigger a 'short-squeeze'.
Investors who short a stock effectively borrow shares and
immediately sell them, hoping to buy them back later at
a lower price, return the borrowed shares and pocket the
profit. Only that's not possible if the share price goes up
because the investor is forced to buy the shares for more than
they borrowed them at, leading to losses for them but a rising
profit for others. And that's exactly what happened. Hot
money rushed into the space and bought GameStop shares
in their droves. At its height, on 28 January 2021, the short-
squeeze caused the stock price to reach $500 per share –
nearly thirty times the $17.25 valuation at the beginning of
the month. Some of the hedge funds that were shorting the
stock took a battering. And this is thought to have been one
of the drivers, anger by retail investors about the practices
of the Wall Street hedge funds and their role in the GFC.
Plus, the democratisation of share trading coupled with retail
trader ability to communicate instantaneously through social
media created a massive hot money bubble.

While the GameStop saga may be an interesting story that
generated documentaries, some online heroes and a few new

millionaires, the impact on the separation of real economy vs financial markets will be felt for many years. Short-selling, when not abused, is a practice that helps markets reflect the fundamental realities of listed companies. The fear of a repeat of the GameStop saga will now be factored into the investment decisions of hedge funds, unwilling to lose their shirts to an unsophisticated yet coordinated group of people, whose main purpose is 'hitting back at Wall Street'. The result: less short-selling taking place, helping to reconnect the equity markets to the real fundamental value of a business in the real economy.

Hot money also had a key role in killing Silicon Valley Bank in 2023. Basically, a mini GFC all over again, only the assets that the SVB held were good quality, not subprime dross. Their problem was that even though the assets were high-quality US treasury bonds, interest rates went up, sending the value of those bonds down. As of 31 December 2022, SVB had mark-to-market accounting unrealised losses in excess of $15 billion for securities held to maturity. In more simple terms, while accounting practices allowed SVB to maintain those securities on the balance sheet at their purchase price, the value on the market was a lot lower. A sudden reduction in deposits would have led the bank to sell those assets on the market, thus realising those losses. And this is exactly what happened. Following a few bad news stories, investors and depositors panicked, and on 9 March 2023 they tried to pull $42 billion from SVB in one of the biggest US bank runs in more than a decade*. SVB's

---

* Weinstein, A., '$42 billion in one day: SVB bank run biggest in more than a decade', *Forbes* (2023).

problems, in a normal environment, were manageable, but the effects of a questionable accounting rule, some negative media coverage and hot money sent it into a tailspin from which it never recovered. SVB was taken over by federal regulators the next day.

Today, the real economy has become overly disconnected from the financial market. The market itself, flooded with money and protected from failure by Central Banks, has boomed.

> ### Today, the real economy has become overly disconnected from the financial market.

This is so much so that it's been very hard to lose money in the stock market over the last decade. But the growth has not been driven by the real economy; it was fuelled by Central Banks, making it very fragile, and many commentators predict that another crash is inevitable until there is systemic change.

Welcome to the Edge of Chaos in Banking

There is little doubt that the disconnect between the financial markets and the real economy has created some incredibly challenging consequences. The resulting fake markets provoke system instability and unsustainability, moving away from an equilibrium of fair resource allocation into the real economy, which in turn, breeds system fragility.

But when a system is unstable, the system *will* find a way to rebalance itself into a new equilibrium. In other words, if the real economy and worthy projects within it do not find the support of the financial and capital markets, they will adjust to use alternative sources of funding and servicing. Digital lending and fintech is the emerging property of a system in transition.

> When a system is unstable, the system *will* find a way to rebalance itself into a new equilibrium. Digital lending and fintech is the emerging property of a system in transition.

This is not just the byproduct of technological progress and innovation, but the universal property of a critical transition of the overall system across what is known as the Edge of Chaos (Figure 1.6).

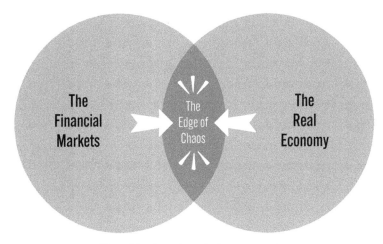

Figure 1.6: The Edge of Chaos in Banking

The Edge of Chaos is a concept used in the study of complex systems, particularly in the field of complexity theory and chaos theory. In the context of complex systems, of which financial systems is one, the Edge of Chaos refers to a critical point between order and chaos and how the most desirable outcome is not complete order or complete chaos but something more sophisticated and perhaps delicate between the two. It is essentially the phase transition space between order and disorder.

Author M. Mitchell Waldrop describes the term as such: *right between the two extremes . . . at a kind of abstract phase transition called the edge of chaos, you also find complexity: a class of behaviours in which the components of the system never quite lock into place, yet never dissolve into turbulence either. These other systems that are both stable enough to store information and yet evanescent enough to transmit it. These are systems that can be organised to form complex computations, to react to the world, to be spontaneous, adaptive, and alive*.

As banks receded from the marketplace, institutional investors have both the need and the opportunity to fill the gap in the real economy. And, in so doing, help real SMEs and real consumers through an array of fintech alternatives. It is these fintech solutions that are being organised to form complex computations that will react to that spontaneous, adaptive and alive world in which we now find ourselves. There is no going back. Banks have gone but banking has not.

A network of data-driven open ecosystems (platforms) is already replacing rigid, top-down centralised structures (banks) in providing funding to the real economy of both unbanked and underbanked businesses and consumers.

The Edge of Chaos is thought to be the locus for evolutionary processes that involve the potential collapse of local structures that then give rise to new patterns of organisation, creating a

---

* Waldrop, M.M., *Complexity: The emerging science at the edge of order and chaos* (Penguin, London, 1994).

dynamic lifecycle*. Waldrop suggests that *The Edge of Chaos is where new ideas and innovative genotypes are forever nibbling away at the edges of the status quo, and where even the most entrenched Old Guard would eventually be overthrown†*. We can already see this happen in banking. The Old Guard is either disappearing or behaving increasingly like Central Banks and not retail or commercial banks.

For more than a decade now, banks have been pulling up the drawbridge to SMEs and consumers in need of working capital financing solutions and retreating to serve only their largest, most lucrative customers. However, we are not just experiencing a substitution of the role traditionally performed by banks, we are also witnessing the complete overhaul of the product suites typical of retail or commercial banking, driven by access to new sources of data in real time. And technology is the lever, enabling the emergence of novel forms of risk underwriting. In addition, being more agile allows digital lenders to offer products tailored to specific sectors and needs.

> For more than a decade now, banks have been pulling up the drawbridge to SMEs and consumers. We are also witnessing the complete overhaul of the product suites typical of retail or commercial banking, driven by access to new sources of data in real time.

It is also worth noting that the idea of the Edge of Chaos is expressed within the work of economist Joseph Schumpeter. Schumpeter proposed a treatise of circular flow, which

---

* Systems Innovation, *The Edge of Chaos*, YouTube (2016).

† Waldrop, M.M., *Complexity: The emerging science at the edge of order and chaos* (Penguin, London, 1994).

excluding any innovations and innovative activity leads to a stationary state. This stationary state is described by Schumpeter as the classical economic equilibrium, of order and predictability. And it is the entrepreneur who disrupts this equilibrium, and is thus the primary cause of economic developments[*].

But what happens when those entrepreneurs in MSMEs and SMEs can't get access to the money they need to disrupt the equilibrium and trigger economic developments?

That's where fintech comes in. Schumpeter also formulated the idea of creative destruction as a driving force within a market economy. Creative destruction describes how new innovations are constantly being generated by entrepreneurs to displace older ones in a continuous cyclical dynamic. Traditional ineffective and sterile financial markets will further drift away from equilibrium (positive feedback loop) and lose relevance in a self-fulfilling, inescapable vicious cycle.

We are already seeing this creative destruction in action with the emergence of embedded finance (more on this in Chapter 3). This disruption is game-changing. Further, tokenisation on the blockchain allows for the conversion of assets into tokens. A major shift will take place from Centralised Finance (Ce-Fi) to Decentralised Finance (De-Fi). Ce-Fi is traditional middle-man orchestrated finance; De-Fi is a world where financial actors interact directly under the overarching rules of cryptographically enforced agreements called smart contracts (more on all this in Chapters 4 and 5). While we are still in the infancy of this movement, certain

---

[*]   Schumpeter, J.A., *The Theory of Economic Development* (Routledge, London, 2021).

benefits can already be seen in action, with the ability to operate on an instant settlement basis (a feat that has never been achieved at scale in the history of finance) and with a level of certainty and transparency that only Distributed Ledger Technology (DLT) can guarantee.

All in all, as fintech platforms, embedded finance, blockchain/De-Fi arise and evolve, the real economy system finds its new equilibrium, away from inefficient and ineffective traditional finance and capital markets. The shadow banking system or alternative finance market comes to the rescue of the traditional commercial banking channel. Prolonged system failures will eventually result in a critical transition of the complex adaptive system of the market into a new equilibrium, where it can better serve the needs of the real economy, thus fostering real productivity while achieving important societal objectives, such as greater equality, in the process. A new stable state will emerge where the system has a new chance to work for everyone, not just the few.

Chapter 2:
Fintech and the Platform Economy

The policies implemented by the Central Banks following the GFC and again during Covid facilitated the conditions that created a massive funding gap. And Fintech is rushing into the void.

Essentially, long-range strategic planning and prudence gave way to short-termism fuelled by astonishing waves of liquidity. Most of us are aware of the government bailouts following the GFC but we are not as familiar with the insane levels of financial stimulus that occurred during the Covid pandemic. These government-backed Covid interventions make the bailouts of 2008 look like chicken feed (Figure 2.1).

Full global lockdowns, endless quantitative easing (QE and QQE), zero or negative interest rate policies (ZIRP or NIRP), modern monetary theory (MMT) and endless government guarantees applied to commercial banks' lending practices have collectively helped to create an entitled society, where the consequences of actions are no longer fully felt by those who perpetuate them. Instead, successive governments and policy-makers have simply bought time. Rather than deal with the systemic issues that their policies have created, they have taken the easy option and kicked those underlying

Fiscal Stimulus: GFC vs COVID ($B)

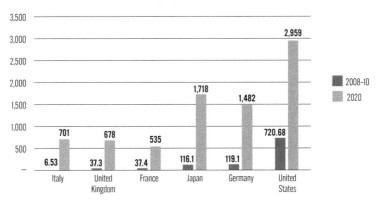

Fiscal Stimulus: GFC vs COVID (% of GDP)

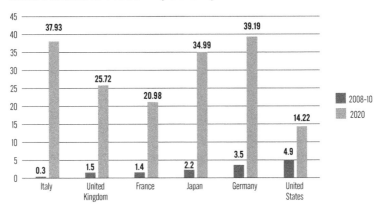

Figure 2.1: Global Stimulus Flooding Markets

Source: McKinsey.com, based on research by the International Monetary Fund (IMF)

problems down the track to be dealt with by someone else or the next government administration.

Short-termism is the utter avoidance of short-term pain, in any way possible and at whatever cost, without much consideration for the immediate impact or the likely long-term consequences – intended or unintended. It is defined by the intentional, often politically motivated choice to swap short-term solutions for long-term problems. This is a conscious choice to secure a win now regardless of the longer-term outcome. Those engaged in short-termism are either unaware that their actions will create other issues down the track or they suspect they might but are happy for someone else to deal with them should they arise. And unfortunately, short-termism is still the underlying virus infecting monetary and fiscal policymaking, and politics at large.

> Short-termism is the utter avoidance of short-term pain, without consideration for the immediate impact or the likely long-term intended or unintended consequences.

In the case of lockdowns, it was understandable. The world was trying to grapple with a global pandemic that was killing millions of citizens. In many ways, not just politically, governments didn't have much choice, but there don't appear to have been very many lessons learned to apply should something similar happen again.

Quantitative easing seems to be the first port of call to solve almost any problem, with Central Banks simply printing more money out of thin air. ZIRPs and NIRPs are supposed to encourage borrowing, spending and investment to stimulate the economy by making the cost of borrowing extremely low or, in the case of NIRPs, actively penalising banks for keeping excess reserves. But persistently low or negative interest rates can pose challenges for financial institutions, particularly banks, as they compress net interest margins. Savers may also be adversely affected and look for alternative homes for their money thus reducing the deposits.

As for MMT, this is a school of thought that emanates from and feeds into the idea of the magic money tree. If there is an economic problem, don't worry, we will just print more money – financial largesse for all with no cost or downside. We are somehow simply entitled to infinite wealth and abundant happiness. It's a bit like giving sweets to a misbehaving child. It may stop the tantrum in the short term but there will be large dentist bills and behavioural issues to deal with down the track.

The unintended consequences of these actions – 'solutions' – are significant. For example, the various waves of liquidity, post-GFC and again during the Covid pandemic, have facilitated the retail-ification of the investor community. Even institutional investors are behaving like retail investors chasing price increases, following trends and engaging in herd mentality rather than taking the long-term view and relying on fundamental analysis and applying shrewd investment insight. Stocks and bonds become so-called 'Giffen Goods', defined by macroeconomics as goods whose demand increases with price. And the reason is simple: markets are now insensitive to risk because of the interventions by the Central Banks and the implicit investor guarantee these interventions have provided.

Against this backdrop, moral hazard is rampant where one party is able to take risks because it does not have to bear the full consequences of those risks. In other words, when individuals or entities are protected from the negative consequences of their actions, they may be more inclined to behave in a riskier manner than they would if they had to bear the full responsibility for the outcomes.

And this is exactly what's happened over a decade or so of somewhat irresponsible monetary policy. Investors have learned and come to expect that, at the first sign of difficulties, the Central Bank will intervene to make sure that markets don't drop too far. This emboldens reckless behaviour, which in turn has resulted in the Bitcoinisation of mainstream markets. 'Bitcoinisation' because people are not buying based on fundamental analysis or rational decision-making but because everyone else is buying! Public markets are moving up in sync all at the same time, both bonds and equities. And when that happens, it may seem like a magic money tree but it's not – at least not for the people who need the money. One cardinal rule gets forgotten in the process. The financial markets exist for one reason: to efficiently allocate capital so that companies that need funding can get funding. This new reality means that the markets are now failing in their core function, fully disconnected from their DNA script.

> Investors have learned and come to expect that, at the first sign of difficulties, the Central Bank will intervene.

It is this failure that has created the funding gap that fintech and the platform economy is plugging. As banks recede, consumers and SMEs are turning to a network of global fintech platforms for the funding they need. And those same institutional investors have a real opportunity to leave the financial market, which is now effectively a casino, and invest in fintech solutions that fill the gap in the real economy. The result is the platformification of credit and the creation of a new form of capital markets.

These platforms are local players within the respective jurisdictions and are able to understand the real needs of the local borrowers, crafting the most efficient, user-friendly experience for them (UX), the most fitting user interface (UI) and the cheapest and fastest solution possible to a very specific borrower requirement in the real economy. Technology is applied where it matters, fully bespoke to the needs of the users and based on local knowledge and experience. This is something banks have not been able to deliver for a long time, as they couldn't always justify the cost and burden of local branches distributed across various global territories. Technology is now leapfrogging that need for physical infrastructure and democratising banking for the first time (more on this in the next chapter).

This is the Edge of Chaos we mentioned in the last chapter. These new platforms and new capital markets are emergent properties in a dynamic financial system that is currently going through a transformation from the old to something completely new (Figure 2.2).

New platforms and new capital markets are emergent properties in a dynamic financial system that is currently going through a transformation from the old to something completely new.

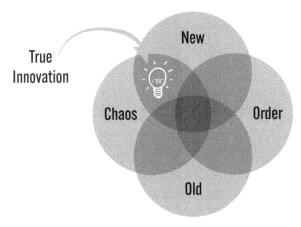

Figure 2.2: True Innovation Needs Chaos

Systems always adjust to survive; the financial system is no different. If the real economy is not getting the funding it needs through the financial markets, then something new will emerge – and has emerged – to meet that need. Emanating from the original sin of short-termism by policy-makers, these new platforms and new capital markets are now filling the gap left by ineffective financial markets and banks who have receded from the SME lending space. Data-driven, resilient and sustainable fintech networks are therefore closing the funding gap in the real economy with capital from institutional investors fleeing 'fugazi markets'.

Fugazi markets are defined by only two factors: chaos and futility. The chaos is baked in because of the polarity of market movements, either slow and incremental or fast and big, the very definition of chaotic behaviour. The futility is also baked into the system because it doesn't matter where a business is in terms of fundamentals. Price discovery is a joke: the S&P could be at 2,000 or 4,000, and it doesn't matter to anyone except the shareholders, as long as the Fed Put is in place.

Savvy institutional investors already know that it's impossible to diversify in fugazi markets because all traditional asset classes move in sync. It's impossible to allocate capital based on merit and fundamentals because the trajectories of those businesses are innately tied to the market movement whether that is fair or valid and accurate or not. The market is essentially a giant casino, and although most sophisticated investors realise this, a lack of alternative investment strategies forces them to the blackjack tables once again. They know that de-anchoring from value puts them in a senseless limbo without purpose – like the dead-eyed gamblers at the roulette wheel, neither euphoric nor devastated at the outcome because none of it matters.

For those who want to either leave the 'casino' and its elitist market bubbles or hedge their investments with some alternative investments, then fintech is that alternative. The system is already rebalancing itself through the creation of a parallel capital market that plugs straight into the real economy, providing a desperately needed service to allow businesses to flourish, triggering real growth in the real economy while also delivering consistent return on investment. True win/win. These alternative non-bank funding solutions are close to reaching mass adoption and are essentially an entirely new asset class running in parallel and as an alternative to equities, fixed income investments, foreign exchange and real estate. And, remember: this asset class is set to meet an unmet global financial need of $7.2 TRILLION dollars globally.

> The system is already rebalancing itself through the creation of a parallel capital market that plugs straight into the real economy.

4th Industrial Revolution

So far, we have experienced four industrial revolutions characterised by transformative changes in the methods of production, technology and societal structures. It's virtually impossible to pinpoint the exact start and end of each revolution and this is still debated by historians and academics. Esteemed historian Eric Hobsbawn believed that the 1st Industrial Revolution began in the UK in the 1780s but wasn't fully felt by wider society until the 1830s or 1840s[*]. Others

---

[*] Hobsbawn, E., *The Age of Revolution: Europe 1789–1848* (Weidenfeld & Nicolson Ltd, London, 1996).

THE FUTURE OF FINANCE

including historian T.S. Ashton believe it occurred earlier, from 1760 to around 1830*. Regardless of the specific dates, this 1st Industrial Revolution was transformational through the introduction of machine-based production using water and steam power. Mechanised textile production and the factory system transformed the UK economy from agrarian, craft-based to an industrial and manufacturing economy and spread to Europe and the US. Later in the period, increased adoption of locomotives, steamboats and steamships made the transport of goods faster and more efficient. The telegraph made a limited appearance around 1840 and rapid economic growth kicked in after 1870, springing from a new group of innovations in what has been called the 2nd Industrial Revolution.

Also known as the technological revolution, this was a period of rapid scientific discovery, including the internal combustion engine, steel-making, chemical engineering, powered flight and electricity. It was also a period of standardisation, mass production and assembly lines running from the late 19th century to the early 20th century. We have the 2nd Industrial Revolution to thank for the widespread adoption of technological systems such as the telegraph. The enormous expansion of rail and telegraph lines facilitated the unprecedented movement of people, products and ideas leading to a new wave of globalisation. The 2nd Industrial Revolution came to an end when World War I broke out in 1914.

The 3rd Industrial Revolution began in the latter half of the 20th century and is also known as the Digital Revolution.

---

* Inikori, J.E., *Africans and the Industrial Revolution in England* (Cambridge University Press, Cambridge, 2002).

This saw a shift from mechanical and analogue electronic technologies toward digital electronics with the adoption and proliferation of computers, microprocessors, digital record-keeping, digital cellular phones and of course the internet. The Information Age had begun.

Today we are in the 4th Industrial Revolution, characterised by the integration of digital technologies from AI, machine learning and gene editing to advanced robotics and the Internet of Things (IoT). The concept of the 4th Industrial Revolution is still evolving, but it represents the ongoing fusion of technologies, blurring the lines between the physical, digital and biological world and is already shaping the way people live and work.

Today we are in the 4th Industrial Revolution, characterised by the integration of digital technologies from AI, machine learning and gene editing to advanced robotics and the Internet of Things (IoT).

Each industrial revolution has marked a significant leap in technological and economic progress, influencing the structure of societies and economies. And when we look at this current 4th Industrial Revolution through the lens of complexity theory, a lot of what is happening makes sense as a system in transition. A system transition at the edge of chaos is in what is known as a 'phase transition zone'. This zone divides a stable system from an unstable system. There are a few common properties of a system in transition and those properties are detectable in the financial markets.

One of the common properties is increased volatility, and if you look at the markets over the last decade, all the monetary and fiscal expansion has created significant volatility (Figure 2.3).

Crisis Times Rising in Magnitude and Speed

Seismograph of Market Activity;
'Sleeping' volcanoes can wake
up faster than thought

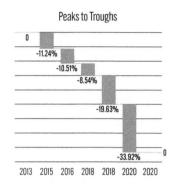

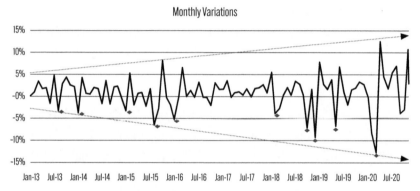

Figure 2.3: Volatility Rising in Magnitude and Speed

Typically, markets have collapsed rapidly when bad news came out. Instant distribution of information, the impact of passive investment strategies and a pervasive herd mentality all contributed to this behaviour. And typically, still deeply influenced by the mistakes and lack of action during the early days of the GFC, Central Banks would rapidly intervene.

In this financial tug of war, volatility is the most apparent and obvious outcome. The monthly variations have been quite dramatic. We believe this is evidence of a system in transition and it is becoming inherently fragile as a result.

In his now famous lecture delivered in December 1972, American mathematician and meteorologist, Edward Lorenz, suggested that 'a butterfly flapping its wings in Brazil can produce a tornado in Texas'. This 'Butterfly Effect' speaks of how very small inputs can cause enormous change. And this is certainly true in the financial markets, where small events can create catastrophic corrections. This fragility is a key part of chaos theory, which Lorenz founded to explain the behaviour of dynamic systems that are highly sensitive to initial conditions.

We are seeing this fragility play out more and more in the financial markets. The market is no longer bouncing back to the way it was but is instead transitioning to a new state. We believe this is already happening and is leading to new capital markets through fintech and blockchain capability.

This transition is also being accelerated because of two additional forces: rising inequality and the technology advancement made possible by the 4th Industrial Revolution (Figure 2.4).

Market Economy System Going Through Critical Transition

Two secular trends intersecting

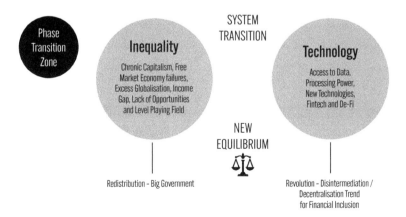

Figure 2.4: Two Trends Accelerating System Transition

Rising Inequality

There is a theory that is popular with policy-makers called 'trickle-down economics'. The idea is that if you make the markets richer, then the wealth that's created will trickle down to everyone else and make everyone else wealthier. This is supposedly achieved by cutting regulation and taxes so that entrepreneurial creativity or 'animal spirit' is unleashed to create more wealth that everyone enjoys through higher wages, for example. Those higher wages are then spent in the economy, creating growth. The problem is, it just doesn't work.

Study after study has shown that tax cuts for wealthy corporations do nothing for the underlying strength of the economy and simply make the already rich, richer. For example, the London School of Economics studied the fiscal policies in eighteen countries over fifty years and concluded that tax cuts for the rich have *never* trickled down and only benefit those directly affected[*].

The last time this approach was tried in the UK was September 2022 when then Chancellor Kwasi Kwarteng, under the 'leadership' of Prime Minister Liz Truss, announced a 'growth plan' mini-budget that included £45 billion of unfunded tax cuts. It was disastrous for the UK economy. Sterling plummeted. The Bank of England was forced into the emergency purchase of government bonds to stabilise the pension market. And it triggered a rise in interest rates to levels not seen since 2008. Both Kwarteng and Truss

---

[*] Reich, R., 'Trickle-down economics doesn't work but build-up does – is Biden listening?' *Guardian* (2020).

were ousted, with Truss becoming the shortest serving prime minister in UK history[*].

In the US, the last time trickle-down economics was implemented as policy was the Tax Cuts and Jobs Act 2017 enacted under President Trump. So, what happed? Walmart, one of the largest employers in the US, saved $2.2 billion a year in tax. They gave employees a $1,000 bonus which was trumpeted in the press, while laying off thousands of staff when they closed sixty-three Sam's Club stores. Technology giant Qualcomm laid off more than 1,500 and did a $10 billion stock buyback which benefited no one except shareholders[†]. Trump assured critics that the tax cuts 'would pay for themselves'. They didn't. Worse, according to the Congressional Budget Office this trickle-down policy added nearly $2 trillion to the federal debt[‡].

This occurs even though we know that wage growth and equality is what drives economic growth. According to Richard Wolff, Professor of Economics Emeritus at the University of Massachusetts, for 100 years up until the 1970s, American capitalism did engage in sustained wage growth. At the time, US capitalism was unique because workers experienced rising real wages year after year. It was this wage growth that created the 'American Dream', allowing the American working class to achieve a standard of living not achieved anywhere else in the world. The driver

---

[*] Islam, F., 'The inside story of the mini-budget disaster', BBC (2023).

[†] Derysh, I., 'Walmart got a $2.2 billion tax cut. Now it's laying off workers', Salon (2019).

[‡] Beyer, D., 'Two Years of Evidence Show 2017 Tax Cuts Failed to Deliver Promised Economic Boost', Joint Economic Committee (2020).

behind this wage growth was a US labour shortage, which meant that employers had to pay good wages and keep increasing those wages to prevent their employees from going elsewhere. This is also what triggered migration to America – people from poorer countries were able to prosper in America.

Wolff states: *The way we* [America] *became a rich, powerful, capitalist country in the 100 years before the 1970s was by providing workers with rising wages**. When employees and ordinary people have more money in their pocket, they spend it. They go out and spend money in restaurants and bars or entertainment venues, they buy new cars or modernise their homes. As a result, that money goes into the real economy to create demand for goods and services and helps businesses prosper and the economy to grow. But when already wealthy people and business owners keep more money via tax cuts, that money is squirrelled away. It's dumped in offshore trust funds to minimise tax still further or it's used in stock buybacks. It never reaches the real economy. All it does is create even greater inequality.

We currently live in a world of the working poor and escalating levels of inequality. The World Inequality Report (2022) describes how *Global wealth inequalities are even more pronounced than income inequalities. The poorest half of the global population barely owns any wealth at all, possessing just 2 percent of the total. In contrast, the richest 10 percent of the global population own 76 percent of all*

---

* KPFA: Wolff, R., 'Capitalism Hits the Fan', YouTube, https://www.youtube.com/watch?v=T9Whccunka4&t=25s [accessed January 2024].

*wealth**. A handful of individuals are wealthier than billions of people! There are 2,640 billionaires (2023) in the world, 735 in the US, and we will probably see the world's first trillionaire in our lifetime, all while huge swaths of the global population are struggling to make ends meet. Apart from being morally questionable, inequality doesn't foster growth and prosperity. Even the IMF has stated that inequality is damaging for economic growth[†].

But there is another type of inequality that is having an even bigger impact on economic growth: corporate inequality. This inequality is certainly as bad if not worse for economic progress. Essentially, it's the difference between the funding available to big companies to expand and take advantage of opportunities and the funding available to small and medium-sized businesses to do the same. As well as acting more like Central Banks, traditional banks who used to be on the high street supporting local businesses and lending to SMEs are no longer interested. They have almost completely receded from that marketplace in favour of the big corporate clients and wealthy individuals and families.

> There is another type of inequality that is having an even bigger impact on economic growth: corporate inequality.

As a result, millions of SMEs struggle to access funding, which is detrimental to the real economy. As mentioned in the last chapter, it is SMEs not big corporates, that contribute

---

* Chancel, L., Piketty, T., Saez, E. and Zucman, G., *World Inequality Report 2022*, World Equality Lab (2022).

† Inman, P., 'IMF study finds inequality is damaging to economic growth', *Guardian* (2014)

to GDP formation and who employ the most people. SMEs are the backbone of the real economy.

In contrast, consider the S&P 500, already an insanely small group of 500 companies that could easily be renamed the S&P 67 because 67 companies are responsible for 85 per cent of the returns in the S&P 500. And even within those 67 companies, just seven companies are responsible for most of that 85 per cent return. By the end of 2023 the S&P 500 was up 21 per cent for the year but without these seven companies, known as the Magnificent Seven on Wall Street, the gains would have been just 6 per cent[*]. The whole system is therefore driven by a tiny handful of extremely successful companies at the top and that's not conducive to distributed financial growth.

We are now reaching a point of redistribution or revolution – perhaps both. In the brilliant book, *The Lessons of History*, authors Will and Ariel Durant conclude that while the concentration of wealth is natural and inevitable, it is periodically alleviated by violent or peaceable partial redistribution.

In Athens of 594 BC for example, when the disparity of fortune between rich and poor had reached its height and the city was ripe for revolution: *The poor, finding their status worsened with each year – the government in the hands of their masters, and the corrupt courts deciding every issue against them – began to talk of violent revolt. The rich, angry at the challenge to their property, prepared to defend themselves by force*[†].

---

[*] Gura, D., 'Wall Street calls them "the Magnificent 7": They're the reason why stocks are surging', npr.org (2023).

[†] Durant, W. and Durant, A., *The Lessons of History* (Simon & Schuster, New York, 1968).

What is so notable and alarming about this story is that we could easily substitute 594 BC for AD 2023 London, Athens, Paris or New York. The anger fomented by inequality certainly remains.

Thankfully for Athens in 594 BC, *Good sense prevailed; moderate elements secured the election of Solon, a businessman of aristocratic lineage, to the supreme archonship. He devalued the currency, thereby easing the burden of all debtors (though he himself was a creditor); he reduced all personal debts, and ended imprisonment for debt; he cancelled arrears for taxes and mortgage interest; he established a graduated income tax that made the rich pay at a rate twelve times that required of the poor; he reorganized the courts on a more popular basis; and he arranged that the sons of those who had died in war for Athens should be brought up and educated at the government's expense. The rich protested that his measures were outright confiscation; the radicals complained that he had not redivided the land; but within a generation almost all agreed that his reforms had saved Athens from revolution*.*

The Romans were not so fortunate. *The Roman Senate, so famous for its wisdom, adopted an uncompromising course when the concentration of wealth approached an explosive point in Italy; the result was a hundred years of class and civil war†.*

It is yet unclear how various governments will choose to deal with this rising inequality in the modern age but, as the Durants go on to say, *In progressive societies the concentration* [of wealth] *may reach a point where the strength of number*

---

* Durant, W. and Durant, A., *The Lessons of History* (Simon & Schuster, New York, 1968).

† Ibid.

in the many poor rivals the strength of ability in the few rich; then the unstable equilibrium generates a critical situation, which history has diversely met by legislation redistributing wealth or by revolution distributing poverty.*

Excessive financial inequality means we are now reaching a point of redistribution or revolution.

The inequality gap has now become so big, so unacceptable and unsustainable that there is little doubt that we are heading for either revolution that distributes poverty or there is sensible legislation that redistributes wealth through altering regulation and taxation.

Capitalism, and the clue is in the name, is designed to provide capital to the real economy. That's the only reason capitalism should exist and yet in its current form it doesn't work. It doesn't get the job done. It doesn't lead to real economic growth and desperately needs to be rethought and reconsidered.

Technology

According to economists Richard Lipsey, Kenneth Carlaw and Clifford Bekar, across the entire span of human history there have been only twenty-four general purpose technologies that have transformed history. These advances have completely altered the economic, political and social landscape over the last 10,000 years and include agriculture

---

* Durant, W. and Durant, A., *The Lessons of History* (Simon & Schuster, New York, 1968).

and the invention of the wheel through to steam engines and the printing press to the computer and the internet.

Although the internet didn't emerge until the 1990s, the idea can be traced back to far earlier. In May 1974, the Institute of Electrical and Electronics Engineers (IEEE) published a paper written by Vint Cerf and Bob Kahn entitled *A Protocol for Packet Network Intercommunication*. It described an Internet Protocol for sharing resources that would become the foundation of the internet we still use today. Every machine has an IP address for example and that relates to this Internet Protocol. Of course, the idea never went anywhere because 1974 was a time when computing power was still the domain of large corporations or organisations that could afford a mainframe computer. Once PCs started to solve that problem in the 1990s, the internet became a reality.

The easiest way to explain the tech revolution that has occurred, largely through the 3rd and 4th Industrial Revolutions, is to look at the changes across Web 1.0, Web 2.0 and Web 3.0 (Figure 2.5).

The Evolution of the Web

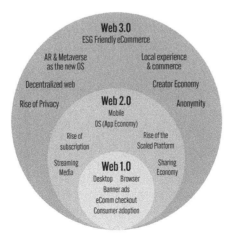

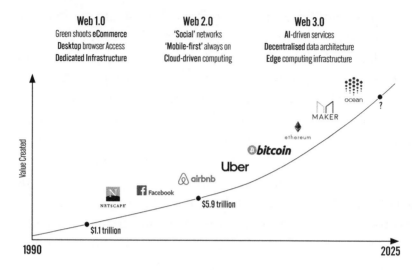

Figure 2.5: The Evolution of the Web

And it has been the connectivity of the internet that has sown the seeds of fintech capability over several decades. Initially, Web 1.0 was just about information exchange. People could get online and view static websites or pages of information or directories. But it was only possible to read that information. This was the era of desktop computers, browsers, banner ads, ecommerce checkouts and search. All that really happened in Web 1.0 was the move from paper-based systems to digital systems on the internet that could then be searched. Over time, Web 2.0 built up around Web 1.0. Internet speeds improved and we moved from dial-up to broadband. Platforms and apps made the user experience better, allowing people to interact and participate online and share content or resources. It was now possible to create audio, visual and written content instead of simply consuming someone else's content. This is the era of social media, for better or worse. It was far easier to use a platform like WordPress to create a professional-looking website than get someone to code the website from scratch. This was the beginning of the sharing economy. Web 3.0 is something very different. Although it is still emerging, it is characterised by increased user control, enhanced privacy, and decentralisation where we don't rely on middlemen and centralised institutions but can access what we need via a vast decentralised network.

Although there has been a tech revolution, exploding with the internet in the 1990s and moving at pace ever since, financial services have, until recently, remained relatively untouched. Corresponding with Web 1.0, fintech 1.0 just offered a better user experience. Although financial services looked different, it was just because it was digital for the first time. Instead of getting paper statements, customers could log on to their bank website and look at their transactions on a screen. They could email their branch and make a request. The fact that the request was actioned by someone at the branch and was not automated was lost on the customer. To them it offered greater convenience and flexibility and so was seen as progress, at least by some.

Fintech 2.0 emerged alongside Web 2.0, where there were apps and financial services platforms for the first time. This was the era of challenger banks such as Revolut or Monzo. These financial service providers didn't have bricks-and-mortar branches; everything was digital native banking on a mobile phone. Fintech 2.0 was made possible largely because of technological advances in smart phones, iPhone and Android. The apps were intuitive, fast and easy to use and the instructions or requests made via the app were automated by the system. The surge in challenger banks during fintech 2.0 was not just down to advancing technological capability but also a backlash against the legacy banking system following the GFC*.

> The surge in challenger banks during fintech 2.0 was not just down to advancing technological capability but also a backlash against the legacy banking system following the GFC.

Changes in regulations also opened the financial services sector making it ripe for innovation (Figure 2.6).

Size: Banks vs Shadow Banks vs Big Tech vs Fintech

Bank and Non-bank Requirements

Bank	Fintech / Non-bank
1. Higher capital requirements (which also require expensive debt and non-tax-deductible preferreds), even on deposits 2. Operational risk capital 3. Extensive liquidity requirements 4. FDIC insurance (this costs JPM ~$12B over the last 10 years - and non-tax-deductible beginning in 2018) 5. UK bank levy and surcharges (this cost JPM ~$3.2B over the last 10 years) 6. More costly regulations (e.g., loans, CFPB, OCC), including resolution planning and CCAR 7. Heavy restrictions around privacy and use of data 8. Extensive KYC / AML requirements 9. Substantial social requirements (CRA) 10. Extensive public and regulatory reporting requirements (e.g., disclosure, compensation) 11. Lower revenue opportunities (e.g., Durbin - this cost JPM ~$17B over the last 10 years)	1. Lower capital requirements, set by market 2. No operational risk capital 3. No liquidity requirements 4. No FDIC insurance 5. No UK bank levy and surcharges 6. Less costly regulations 7. Fewer privacy restrictions, virtually no data restrictions 8. Less extensive KYC / AML requirements 9. No social requirements (CRA) 10. Limited public and regulatory reporting requirements 11. Higher debit card income FDIC = Federal Deposit Insurance Corporation CFPB = Consumer Financial Protection Bureau OCC = Office of the Comptroller of the Currency CCAR = Comprehensive Capital Analysis and Review KYC = Know Your Customer AML = Anti-money laundering CRA = Community Reinvestment Act

Figure 2.6: Bank vs Non-Bank Requirements

---

* Cooke, G.C., *Web3: The End of Business as Usual* (Whitefox, London, 2022).

There is little doubt that this regulatory change has disadvantaged the legacy banking system. In his annual letter to shareholders in 2022, J.P. Morgan Chase CEO Jamie Dimon lamented the lack of a level playing field between banks and fintech operators, adding: *The growing competition to banks from each other, as well as shadow banks, fintechs and large technology companies, is intense and clearly contributing to the diminishing role of banks and public companies in the United States and the global financial system. The pace of change and the size of the competition are extraordinary, and activity is accelerating. Walmart, for example (with over 200 million in-store customers each week), can use new digital technologies to efficiently bring banking-type services to their customers. Apple, already a strong presence in banking-type services with Apple Pay and the Apple Card, is actively moving into other similar services such as payment processing, credit risk assessment, person-to-person payment systems, merchant acquiring and buy-now-pay-later offers. Large tech companies, already 100 percent digital, have hundreds of millions of customers, as well as enormous resources, in data and proprietary systems — all of which give them an extraordinary competitive advantage*[*].

It is, however, a little ironic that legacy banks are now complaining about a lack of level playing field when they have enjoyed *their* privilege for centuries. The GFC shook that privilege, and legacy banking took a massive reputational hit. Stories of greed and hubris, not to mention the real-world financial pain it created for many ordinary people, eroded

---

[*] Dimon, J., *Annual Report 2022*, https://reports.jpmorganchase. com/investor-relations/2022/ar-ceo-letters.htm

trust in banks. Plus, the ramifications of the GFC meant that changes to the regulation were necessary so that new players could meet the needs of customers the banks were no longer willing or able to meet.

It is easy to see why traditional banks feel so threatened. Banks are playing an increasingly smaller role in the financial system. Because of advances to technology and changing regulation, we are witnessing a massive growth in shadow banks or non-banking entities offering banking solutions (Figure 2.7).

Size: Banks vs Shadow Banks vs Big Tech vs Fintech

Size of the Financial Sector/Industry

($ in trillions)		2000	2010	2020
Size of banks	US banks market capitalisation	1.2	1.3	2.2
	US GSIB market capitalisation	0.9	0.8	1.2
	European banks market capitalisation	1.1	1.5	1.1
	US bank loans	3.7	6.6	10.5
	Total U.S. broker dealer inventories	2.0	3.5	3.7
	US bank common equity	0.4	1.0	1.5
	US bank liquid assets	1.1	2.8	7.0
Market size	Total US debt and equity market	33.6	57.2	118.4
	Total US GDP	13.3	15.8	18.8
Shadow banks	Total private direct credit	7.6	13.8	18.4
	Total US passives and ETFs	6.9	13.6	30.8
	Total US money market funds	1.8	2.8	4.3
	Hedge fund and private equity AUM	0.6	3.0	8.0
Size of evolving competitors	Google, Amazon, Facebook, Apple	NM	0.5	5.6
	Payments	NA	0.1	1.2
	Private and public fintech companies	NA	NA	0.8
Sources: FactSet. S&P Global Market Intelligence, Federal Reserve Z.1, Federal Reserve H.8, Preqin and Federal Reserve Economic Data (FRED) GSIB = Global Systemically Important Banks NA = Not applicable NM = Not material				

Figure 2.7: Banks vs Shadow Banks vs Big Tech vs Fintech

It is easy to see why traditional banks feel so threatened. Banks are playing an increasingly smaller role in the financial system.

Fintech essentially sits at the intersection between financial services and technological innovation (Figure 2.8).

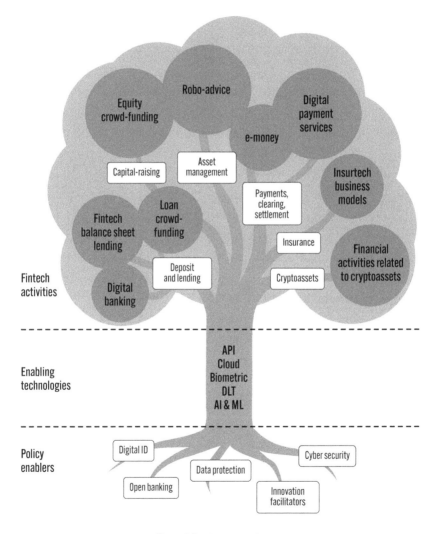

Figure 2.8: The Fintech Tree

The roots of the tree are the changes in regulation and various policy enablers. The trunk of the tree is the enabling technologies such as APIs, cloud capability, biometric security and advances in AI. Collectively, they have created a smorgasbord of fintech outputs, which we will explore shortly.

Fintech 3.0 is decentralised finance running on Web 3.0 apps and platforms. And the financial system will transition into a new equilibrium of fintech lending and digital assets.

What makes these iterations of fintech so exciting is the stability, return on investment and the value these services are delivering *to the real economy*. Where traditional banking is funded by deposits, fintech businesses are backed by private capital (both debt and equity). Banks funded by deposits have already been shown to be extremely vulnerable to financial contagion. This new parallel capital market avoids that risk and it is seen as one of the key elements of resilience in the sector, offering investors a genuine alternative to the fragility of the current financial markets.

The Fintech Revolution

Fintech innovation goes far beyond the simple online conversion of the traditional banking offerings such as savings and lending. It is further evolved by the creation and management of electronic currencies such as Bitcoin and other blockchain networks that are enabling the birth of new business models. Just as the internet was transformative for the mobility of information, digital assets will be revolutionary for the way in which value is transferred. We are witnessing entirely new financial rails being engineered in real time, which will be able to handle users at scale.

Individuals and small business owners, whether they don't want to visit a branch, or no longer have a local branch to visit, are seeking different ways of meeting their financial needs. And the different way is by going online or opening an app on their phone and accessing new fintech-enabled marketplaces.

This app or portal will give them access to all sorts of digital lending options. The list is vast and growing every day. It already includes all of the capabilities below, with new products being added and developed on a regular basis:

- **Receivables True Sales (Disclosed):** an advance against an outstanding customer invoice. A flexible solution that does not require to sell all customer invoices. Each transaction is disclosed to the debtor.
- **Receivables True Sales (Undisclosed):** an advance against an outstanding customer invoice. A flexible solution that does not require to sell all customer invoices. Each transaction is undisclosed to the debtor.
- **Trade Finance:** an advance against outstanding customer invoices in the international commodity trading sector. Transactions usually benefit from credit insurance and are executed after the shipment of goods.
- **Supply Chain Finance:** advances against outstanding customer invoices to a large established corporate entity. The agreement usually involves a large company and its network of suppliers, which can benefit from advances on all the invoices issued by the company.
- **Promissory Notes/Bills of Exchange:** advances against documents (promissory notes or bills of exchange), usually related to international transactions.

- **Purchase Order Financing:** short-term loans (up to 180 days) for the payment of a specific supplier invoice.
- **Unsecured SME Loans:** fully amortised loans to SMEs with monthly repayments.
- **Secured SME Loans:** fully amortised loans to SMEs with monthly repayments. Loans are secured against collateral (property, inventory, equipment, etc.).
- **Merchant Cash Advance:** cash advances against a percentage of future revenues of the business (generally a retailer) generated through traceable payment methods (i.e. credit / debit cards).
- **Real Estate Development Loans (Residential):** bullet loans to small real estate developers typically with a duration between 6 and 24 months for the execution of residential development projects, secured with a mortgage on the underlying properties.
- **Buy-to-Let Loans:** loans to a landlord for the acquisition of property to be let and secured with a mortgage.
- **Commercial Real Estate Loans:** bullet or amortised loans with a duration up to 60 months and secured with a mortgage on a commercial property.
- **Mortgages:** amortised loans secured by a mortgage on an already existing residential property.
- **Direct Loans:** fully amortised loans to consumers with monthly repayments and duration up to 60 months.
- **Credit Cards:** advances against consumer credit card balances originating through third-party credit card operators.
- **Car Leasing:** advances against car leasing contracts with a duration typically up to 60 months.
- **Tech Leasing:** advances against consumer electronics, leasing contracts with a duration up to 24 months.

- **Instalment Financing:** financing of very short-term and low-value consumer credit card receivables up to 60 days originating through buy-now-pay-later financial products.
- **Student Loans:** advances against short-term loans to fund training and education typically with a duration up to 12 months.
- **Revenue Based Lending:** cash advanced against a percentage of future revenue. Unlike merchant cash advances, the asset class focuses on technology companies in their early stage and represents a complementary source of funding alongside equity raises.
- **App Development Financing:** short-term advances to app developers against earned credit on app distribution platforms. Typically takes the form of a revolving facility with short-term repayments cycles (30–45 days).
- **Medical Expenses Financing:** consumer financing at a point of sale for medical treatment (such as dental treatment) and monthly instalments up to 36 months.
- **Point of Sale Financing:** loans originated at time of purchase of a good or asset, typically with a duration up to 36 months.

For example, if a business owner needs capital, they can bypass the bank and use an online website to secure an advance against their receivables. They effectively sell some of their outstanding invoices to a third-party fintech provider who will take a percentage of the receivables but provide the rest of the money upfront.

Instead of buying a car at a local dealership you could go online, select the car you want to use, provide an address where the car will be delivered and set up a subscription for a monthly payment of the car. The same can be done with tech leasing. If you get sick of your iPhone you can just swap it out for a laptop or iPad. These types of offers are incredibly flexible and are very popular, especially with the younger generation who likes the 'no strings attached' freedom of the deal. It also taps into the circular or shared economy, where people are far happier to rent something for a short period of time than be tied into ownership over the long term. Not only is it more convenient but this approach is more respectful of the environment and avoids waste. These lending options are offering borrowers a better, faster, cheaper and frictionless experience. And they are winning hands down against the commercial banks.

Technology such as blockchain (more on that in the next chapters) has also given rise to innovative digital assets. In just a single decade, digital assets have been able to accumulate more than a trillion dollars' worth of market capitalisation on exchanges and the blockchain in general and, while estimates vary substantially depending on the source, NFTs alone were able to capture tens of billions in market cap. These are very big numbers.

To give another sense of the magnitude of these numbers, Revolut, one of the most successful challenger banks, has around 10 million accounts. But there are already well over a billion accounts on the blockchain!

The result is the emergence of the platform economy, a new economic system in which digital platforms facilitate and mediate exchanges between users. These platforms serve as intermediaries that connect buyers and sellers, service providers and consumers or other participants in an open-source, decentralised marketplace. These transactions may involve goods, services or information. The platforms in this new economy will collect and analyse large amounts of data generated by user interactions. This data will be used to improve the platform's services, enhance user experience and inform business strategies. Users will actively contribute to the platform by creating content, providing reviews and engaging in transactions. And these platforms will be able to generate revenue through various monetisation models, such as transaction fees, subscription fees, advertising or data monetisation.

> The result is the emergence of the platform economy, a new economic system in which digital platforms facilitate and mediate exchanges between users.

Not only will this model revolutionise finance but it will also play an important part in the redistribution of wealth.

Chapter 3:
The Future of Embedded Fintech

If we look back at the trajectory of technological advance, how it has developed and how it has therefore been used in business over several decades, we can see an evolution from simple use in dedicated departments to technology becoming a core functionality of every company, central to that company's competitive advantage. We believe finance, and specifically fintech, is following the same trajectory.

We hinted at this change in the opening chapter, but it's worth revisiting the story to unpack the evolution that took technology from being a component part of business delivered by an 'IT' department to being central to the operation and profitability of every department in every business.

In 1975, when Robert was running Owen's Shoes, the business was relatively untouched by technology. Robert was always interested in ways to improve his business, so he read widely and was aware of some of the latest developments. He knew, for example, that mainframe computers had been invented in the 1960s. Although powerful and viewed as a revelation at the time, their use was limited to very large companies with very deep pockets. The early mainframes were huge and extremely expensive but they offered a range of capabilities including data processing, batch processing, storage and retrieval, database management and early networking that offered the companies that could afford a mainframe a distinct competitive advantage.

To make this expensive hardware more efficient, time-sharing was invented in the 1970s which allowed each mainframe to be used by multiple people at the same time. This was a game-changing innovation and an early version of the cloud computing capability we take for granted today.

Robert's day-to-day activity was very analogue. He operated a mechanical till and if he needed to contact a supplier, he would either write a letter on his typewriter or consult his address book, find the contact details of the supplier and call them. Of course, the 1970s were the days when people remembered phone numbers, so he knew his main suppliers' numbers off by heart.

Robert was not unusual. Most businesses during the 1970s and even most of the 1980s operated manual analogue systems. The technologies that were emerging, such as mini computers, word processors, modems, networking capabilities and early bar coding were all still expensive and only the largest companies could afford to invest in them. Besides, none of these advances were particularly relevant to Robert's business. He did invest in an electronic cash register in the mid-1980s but that was about it. He really didn't need anything else and whilst he was interested in what was happening, the costs were prohibitive.

By the mid-1990s he'd also invested in a personal computer (PC). Although PCs emerged in the very early days of the 1970s, they didn't really saturate the market until the late 1980s and 1990s. Robert, like millions of others, bought an IBM PC with a Microsoft operating system. It allowed him to get rid of his typewriter, accounts ledger and address book as he transferred that information to his PC.

Of course, by the mid-1990s Robert had heard about the internet – who hadn't? Back in 1980, physicist Tim Berners-Lee created a prototype for a system that would be used by CERN researchers to share documents. Ten years later he wrote the browser and server software for hypertext markup language better known as HTML. HTML was a revelation because it allowed for the visualisation of information on a computer. Up until this point, everything on a computer, mainframe or PC was text-based. HTML allowed individuals and businesses to create digital pages that included images, text, colour and buttons. This extended the use and functionality of technology beyond text or number-based tasks carried out in the accounts or administrative departments, for example, into the creative departments of business, such as advertising and marketing. As such, technology advanced significantly as an embedded function, necessary in more and more aspects of business operation.

The advent of HTML and the internet made it possible for Robert to create a digital shopfront online, which could act like a printed brochure advertising his products to a far wider audience than his local community. And whilst Robert recognised the potential, like many business owners at the time, he didn't have time to invest in the technology. Luckily, he had an inquisitive daughter. Prior to her final year at university, Libby was home for summer so Robert asked her to investigate the internet and see how easy it would be to set up an Owen's website. Every morning, Libby would come to the shoe store with her dad and hop on the PC to research and explore the burgeoning internet.

Robert had upgraded his PC to a Dell machine running

Windows 95, giving him access to Windows Office which included Word, Excel, PowerPoint, Access Database and Microsoft Mail. He'd bought a modem and had set up an email account with AOL a few years earlier, so he would use dial-up connection to get online and check his email, but he hadn't found the time to do any more.

Dial-up internet connection was very clunky, took several minutes to connect and was notoriously unstable. Every day, Libby would remind her dad not to use the phone when she was online. Every day, he would forget and she would be subjected to screeching, hissing and buzzing as she was booted offline! Her dad would apologise and she would attempt to connect again. Once online, Libby found websites that, by today's standards, were hideous, but they were still a revelation and she could immediately see that the internet had huge potential for the business.

Every evening, she would share what she had found with her dad over dinner and they would plot how best to use this innovation.

During the 1970s, 1980s and to a lesser extent the 1990s, technology was either only available to the largest, wealthiest businesses or it was a piecemeal solution to a particular challenge. The role of technology for most SMEs for example was largely to digitise analogue processes, typed letters to email, paper ledgers to spreadsheets, card files to databases and the ability to store and sort data. And these innovations certainly delivered greater accuracy and saved time and money. For larger businesses there might have been an 'IT Department', but their role was usually just to keep the technology working.

The innovations that pushed the internet beyond a replacement for the analogue system into something completely new was probably high-speed broadband connections, cloud computing and the smartphone.

Although Libby built an HTML website for her dad and used it as the case study for her university dissertation, it was very basic. Slow dial-up internet connection put most customers off, it was still just easier to visit a store. So, even with a website, Owen's Shoes didn't suddenly transform into an online retailer. There was no cost-effective way to process payments, so the website was little more than a static digital brochure.

But by the time Libby was running the business in 2013, things were *very* different. Technology was no longer simply a department in large organisations that assisted in storing and processing data, it was a core element of competitive advantage at every level. The initial HTML website had been upgraded to a full-service ecommerce site where people could browse shoes, double check their shoe size with an online tool, order and pay for their shoes and have them delivered to their door. Libby knew what her customers bought, had data on their purchasing habits and could tailor her digital marketing strategy accordingly. She used cloud computing capability and data analytics to extract the most insight and value from the data she held on her customers and this gave her far greater predictability over sales.

The breakthrough that triggered the cloud computing revolution occurred in 2003. Xen, a Cambridge University research project, worked out how to allow multiple operating systems to execute on the same computer hardware at the same time. This had always been an issue since the mainframe computers of the 1960s: how to squeeze as much efficiency out of expensive hardware. Xen found the solution that allowed for the virtual sharing of every component part of the machine, capable of running hundreds of operating systems and processes at the same time, all connected through a network.

In the US, Xen's innovation proved very interesting to Amazon's chief technical officer (CTO), Werner Vogels. At the time he was looking for greater efficiencies in the Amazon network. His problem was that since the inclusion of third-party sellers via Amazon Marketplace in 2000, traffic to Amazon had increased significantly. Although a good problem to have, it meant that Amazon needed huge banks of computers to manage the spikes in orders that occurred around particular sales events or holidays and the excess capacity would then sit idle during the normal trading periods. Vogels knew what Xen had achieved and was able to create a cloud solution: Amazon Web Services (AWS). This effectively became a separate Amazon business and in 2021 it generated $62.2 billion in revenue[*].

Cloud computing took a while to catch on. Businesses tended to live inside a technological walled garden and didn't initially like the idea of a shared data storage space. But, over time and with reassurances about security, cloud capability became a huge area of competitive advantage for business. Increased storage space coupled with big data analytics have made it possible for companies to assess customer data, predict buying patterns and so much more.

As for the smartphone, it too was a game-changer because it effectively put a computer in someone's pocket and high-speed broadband connection meant that people could get online 24/7. When Steve Jobs launched the iPhone in January

---

[*] Goldberg, J., 'Amazon Reveals Its Most Profitable Business', *Forbes* (2022).

2007 it was like nothing anyone had seen before. Before the iPhone, mobile phones were 'bricks', the most popular being the Nokia 5110. It's hard to imagine now but Nokia used to dominate the mobile phone market. Everyone had a Nokia and yet the most interesting thing it could do was send an SMS message. The iPhone, on the other hand, had a multi-touch interface, allowing users to interact with the device by tapping, pinching and swiping. It had access to Safari web browser via 2G connectivity, it included the iPod music functionality as well as the expected phone, messaging and camera capabilities. That first iPhone, that could comfortably fit in your pocket and cost around $500, was 412 times faster than the early mainframes, which were so huge they had their own rooms and cost millions of dollars. The latest iPhone is 3,100 times faster than the early mainframes*!

By the time Libby is running Owen's, 100 per cent of the business processes makes use of technology. Thanks to high-speed internet, Libby can sell products online, showing them with high-resolution pictures. And she can also find suppliers through B2B marketplaces. Thanks to cloud computing, she can manage the finances of her business through third-party software that allows her to deploy algorithms that only a few years earlier were only available to the largest global technology players. This means she can estimate what to order and when, what the financial needs of the business will be and what actions to take to improve the results of her business. And thanks to the smartphone, she is in control 100 per cent of the time. Even while on holiday, she can

---

* Piui, T., 'Your smartphone is millions of times more powerful than the Apollo 11 guidance computers', ZME Science (2023).

check the business bank account and make payments, she can review online sales and send quick emails or messages to her suppliers. We can easily say that technology permeates her business and those of millions of small and large entrepreneurs like her, all over the world.

If left to his own devices, Robert, Libby's dad, would have loved to invest in some of the technology that was emerging in the 1980s, and early 1990s, but the initial versions were too expensive and often glitchy. They didn't work seamlessly and business owners don't usually have the time or inclination to be beta testers when their livelihood is on the line, especially not SMEs. For example, it didn't make sense for Robert to 'go online' and use word processing or spreadsheet products when they were far less useful and effective than the off-line Windows product suite. Robert, like millions of business owners, needed stuff to work and work well, straight out of the box.

The tech revolution that converted technology to an embedded capability was therefore only possible when the costs dropped and the functionality increased, making it not only affordable but reliable and accessible. Business owners tend not to be innovators or even early adopters, they wait until the technology has 'crossed the chasm' and then get involved. It was organisational theorist and author Geoffrey A. Moore who noticed that there was a 'chasm' between the people who rushed to get into technology and the mass market. Only when technology had crossed the chasm to the mass market did it become ubiquitous[*]. That is the position

---

[*]   Moore, G.A., *Crossing the Chasm: Marketing and selling disruptive products to mainstream customers* (3rd edn, Harper Business, New York, 2014).

we are in now, which has transformed technology from something located in a department or used for discrete tasks to an embedded part of business operations and a source of competitive advantage.

The tech revolution that converted technology to an embedded capability was only possible when the costs dropped and the functionality increased.

We will explore in more detail in the next two chapters the capabilities that are already here and the fintech lending and digital assets innovations that will be available to business as part of a rich network of embedded finance solutions, but it is important to recognise the parallels between how technology has evolved from being a component of some businesses to being an embedded aspect for every business. Technology is now embedded into all aspects of every business whether that business is a concrete factory, a plumber or a consultancy. We believe the same thing will happen in finance. The trend is just at the beginning.

For decades, technology was only ever delivered by a handful of dominant players including IBM, Dell, HP, Microsoft, Apple and Oracle, but innovation opened the market and new players rushed into the gaps left by the main players. The same thing is happening in finance. For centuries, finance was only ever delivered by a handful of dominant banks in each jurisdiction. A global financial crash, the erosion of trust and changes to regulation have also opened the market and new fintech players are rushing into the gaps left by banks receding from their traditional markets. Remember, fintech exists at the intersection between technology and finance, but the technology component is shifting the balance of power in finance from *only* banks to include an array of non-bank players.

This shift means that when a business needs access to money they have new options in the form of plug-and-play apps and platforms that every business will be able to use. Their function will not be limited to accessing money when needed but these tech-enabled capabilities will allow every company to offer what were traditionally banking services to their network of clients, thus providing a new way to find and make money in the business.

For centuries banks were the bastions of finance, the trusted third party that would provide money to individuals and businesses alike, helping to fund and grow the real economy. Legacy systems and regulatory protection ensured their monopoly over finance but a series of events, laid out in earlier chapters, together with a surge in technological innovation has completely changed the financial landscape.

The 3Ds

There is little doubt that technological advance is playing a significant role in the divergence of the finance industry. Just as technology went from being a tool for specific tasks to an embedded capability in every department of every business, finance, or the access and use of money, will become an embedded capability inside every business.

Three aspects to this technological revolution are facilitating this sea change:

- Digitisation
- Democratisation
- Decentralisation

Digitisation

Web 1.0, or the first iteration of the internet, was essentially just the conversion of analogue information to a digital format on the World Wide Web and made available to others via the internet. This capability has meant an explosion of not only the volume of information that is now available digitally but the type of information that is held digitally and how it can be used.

In 1981, nine years before web-anything, futurist and inventor R. Buckminster Fuller proposed 'the knowledge doubling curve'. Fuller suggested that the more knowledge we accumulated, the faster we created even more knowledge. For example, up until 1900, human knowledge doubled every hundred years or so. By the end of World War II, the complete knowledge of mankind is thought to have doubled every twenty-five years. By 1982 knowledge was doubling every twelve to thirteen months[*]. In 2006, IBM predicted that knowledge would double every eleven hours by 2010[†]. It's unclear if that rate has been reached or even surpassed, but what is undisputed is that we now have access to more information, knowledge and data than ever before. Most of that information has been digitised and is available to us via the internet. Eighteen million gigabytes of data are added to the global sum of all data every single minute of every day[‡]. It is so vast that it would take us 28.3 million years or hundreds of thousands of lifetimes to

---

[*]   Sorokin, S., 'Thriving in a World of "Knowledge Half-Life"', CIO (2019).

[†]   IBM Global Technology Services, 'The Toxic Terabyte: How data dumping threatens business efficiency' (2006).

[‡]   Sulleyman, M. and Bhasker, M., *The Coming Wave* (Vintage, London, 2023).

read everything that is currently on the internet[*]. And that is not including everything that is not.

With the help of cloud computing and data analytics, businesses are now able to use that data to extract important insights on everything from productivity to buying patterns. It's one thing to have information, but it only really becomes useful when it can be analysed. Before cloud computing, that simply wasn't possible for anyone except the largest companies – no one else could afford the necessary hardware. Cloud computing and advances in processing power and speed put this capability into the hands of every business. Advances in big data, machine learning, analytics and AI provide very powerful tools to everyone, including SMEs, as they seek to carve out a competitive advantage in their market (more on these in the next chapter).

When business has access to these tools, they can start to see patterns of behaviour or areas for greater efficiency that are impossible to see with smaller datasets. Assumptions, expectations and 'best guesses' give way to probability and predictability. When customers buy certain products, for example, the data can predict what else might be needed and advertise accordingly. US retailer Target got into hot water over its big data algorithms when a school-age girl was sent discount vouchers for baby products. Her parents complained, only to discover a few days later that she was in fact pregnant, it's just that Target knew before they did – because of patterns identified in the data[†].

----

[*] Gibson, J., 'How long would it take to browse the entire internet?' Quora (2016).

[†] Duhigg, C., 'How Companies learn your secrets', *The New York Times* (2012).

What's astonishing is that when Fuller first hypothesised about knowledge doubling there was no internet, no smart phones, no PCs or laptop computers, no satellite TV, no smart sensors, limited artificial intelligence and no social media.

But it's not just the volume of digitised data, it's the forms of data that can now be digitised that offer new possibilities. Everything creates or can yield data in a constant 'datafication' of our world. It's no longer limited to words, numbers or images but includes other types, such as data from sensors. All are now available for collection and analysis.

> Everything creates or can yield data in a
> constant 'datafication' of our world.

Take Rolls-Royce as an example. The company powers thirty-five different types of commercial aircraft and has over 13,000 engines in service around the world. But data has allowed them to transition from a manufacturing company to a service company, where they use cloud-based technologies to analyse hundreds of data points coming in from each engine in the air – every second. The performance of each engine is modelled in the cloud using real-time engine data from its customers, with the aim of reducing unnecessary maintenance and unplanned time on the ground for planes. Not only is this saving customers money but Rolls-Royce have already saved 22 million tons of carbon, using the data feeds from planes in flight while providing guidance to pilots on how to fly their planes better[*].

---

[*] du Preeze, D., 'How Rolls-Royce is improving engine sustainability with real-time data and digital twins', diginomica (2021).

There are now far more things collecting more types of digitised data than people on the planet and increasingly they are being connected via the Internet of Things (IoT), a vast network of physical devices, vehicles, appliances and other objects with sensors, software, and network connectivity. The number of IoT devices worldwide is forecast to almost double from 15.1 billion in 2020 to more than 29 billion by 2030*. This network will allow for the collection and exchange of data which has the potential to bring about significant advancements in efficiency, automation and decision-making across diverse sectors – including finance.

Why is this so relevant for fintech? Before the internet and cloud computing, data held by a business was considered sacred and walled off from the outside world in closed systems. Now, each business has the ability to collect more data and can choose to share parts of that information for the purpose of accessing a financial service such as obtaining a loan. But instead of digging out the data and including it with a loan application, the data exchange can be done automatically, in real time, in the platform economy. Digitalisation is therefore allowing fintech companies to tear down the information barriers that, for decades, made it impossible to compete with traditional banks.

This widespread and far-reaching digitisation has also made it possible to dematerialise assets, making them far easier to trade. And we have already seen incredible innovation in this space.

---

* No Author, 'Number of Internet of Things (IoT) connected devices worldwide from 2019 to 2023, with forecasts from 2022 to 2030', Statistica (2023).

Fractionalisation, a subset of digitisation, is also having tremendous impact. It allows people to invest in fractions of assets, reducing the minimum capital required and creating novel investment opportunities for everybody. Fractionalisation covers both traditional assets such as equities and bonds as well as alternative assets such as art, collectibles and real estate. In 2010 owning a Picasso was only possible for a miniscule percentage of the world population. Today, through your smartphone, you can acquire a small fraction of a painting worth millions of dollars and profit from its sale at auction. We will explore this in more detail in Chapter 5.

Democratisation

Democratisation means making something accessible to everyone. How can something be made more accessible? You need to make it cheaper and easier to find and use! And the best way to make a product cheaper and easier to find and use is to create an ecosystem where competition increases, driving the most expensive, less efficient players out of the market. Technology, in this regard, plays a crucial role both at the micro level and at the macro level.

At the micro level, we can look at digitisation as a key enabler of democratisation. Digital data is easier to store than physical data; it is much easier to process and easier to transfer. The cost associated with dealing with data today is a tiny fraction of what it was twenty-five years ago. And while data was being digitised, algorithms for analysing and interpreting the data became accessible to everybody through cloud computing and 'software-as-a-service' (SaaS) offerings. In other words, the cost of accessing technology and innovation plummeted and allowed smaller players to start challenging the legacy operators and offer services to areas of the market that were previously considered unprofitable to serve.

At a macro level, technological advance is also creating far more equality between the developed and developing world. For example, in developed countries a robust legacy telecommunication infrastructure allowed the owners of that infrastructure to maintain lucrative monopoly positions and slow down progress for decades. But those same robust infrastructures don't always exist in developing countries. The advent of smart phones and mobile communication meant it no longer mattered. In Africa or India business owners have simply leapfrogged the old landline infrastructure and gone straight to digital and smart phone technologies at a fraction of the cost. Many SMEs in the developing world are conducting business very efficiently via a smartphone and a stable internet connection! In those markets, fintech are not just substituting legacy financial institutions, but in certain cases pioneering the development of new products and services in completely untapped markets.

Easier, more user-friendly, access to technology is also allowing business owners to reduce the point at which a customer relationship becomes profitable. In addition, access to enriched data and the use of AI improves credit assessment and allows fintechs to offer services to a client base that has normally been ignored because of the difficulty in assessing their creditworthiness – again, making huge strides in addressing the inequality that currently exists in finance.

> Easier, more user-friendly access to technology is also allowing business owners to reduce the point at which a customer relationship becomes profitable.

The biggest hurdle to these developing countries is not the lack of access to tech per se, it's access to high-speed internet. Take Africa as an example. Africa is home to 1.4 billion people, nearly one in five people on the planet live in Africa and yet 57 per cent of the African population doesn't have a bank account or mobile wallet. In 2020, Africa's total financial services market revenue totalled $150 billion. By 2025, it's expected to reach over $230 billion. That's a massive pie. But right now, access to high-speed stable internet varies from 84.1 per cent in Morocco to 17.6 per cent in the Democratic Republic of Congo*. The fastest way to democratise finance and indeed anything else in Africa and other developing nations is to provide stable, reliable, high-speed broadband connection.

Decentralisation

The third aspect that is facilitating the changes we are witnessing not only in technology but also finance is the concept of decentralisation. Decentralisation refers to the distribution of authority, control or computing resources across a network, rather than being concentrated in a central location or controlled by a single entity. For centuries, finance has been controlled by individual entities – banks – but that is now changing. Instead, new systems are being designed or networks created that minimise reliance on a single point of control or failure.

Experimentations with decentralisation started in the early 2000s with peer-to-peer (P2P) lending, an innovative,

---

* Masako Welch, E., 'The Future of Fintech in Africa', Special Report, Entrepreneur and Lucidity Insights (2023).

tech-enabled approach to connecting those who needed capital with those who had capital to lend. Also known as crowdfunding or social lending, the concept of P2P lending involves individuals lending and borrowing money directly from one another through online platforms, bypassing traditional financial institutions like banks.

The P2P lending model gained momentum through the 2000s, with the establishment of various platforms globally. Notable examples include LendingClub, founded in 2006 in the US and Funding Circle, founded in 2010 in the UK. It has continued to evolve, offering different types of loans, including personal loans, business loans and student loans and we will unpack this in more detail in the next chapter.

However, P2P lending is only decentralised in so far as it has by-passed the banks. In other words, the process of lending is very similar, it's just that someone other than a bank is making the decisions. The real game-changer, when it comes to decentralisation, was the invention of the blockchain.

A blockchain is a decentralised and distributed digital ledger that records transactions across a network of computers. It is designed to be secure, transparent and resistant to modification. The blockchain consists of a chain of digital blocks, where each block contains a list of transactions. These blocks are linked together in a chronological order, forming a continuous chain. You can think of a blockchain like a journal. Each page of the journal (a block) contains notes related to transactions and all the blocks are ordered in the journal through the indication of the page number at the bottom. But this is a magic journal. Every time you enter a new page, this automatically appears in the journal of hundreds of thousands of people around the world and they all need to reach a consensus in approving those transactions.

This makes it impossible to forge the journal, making it much more reliable than any centralised system. Though that process seems cumbersome and unrealistic, if you move from a physical journal to a digital one, everything is faster and more reliable. At the time of writing, a new block on the Ethereum blockchain is minted every twelve seconds.

We will explore blockchains in more depth in Chapter 5 but, for now, the primary advantage is decentralisation, eliminating the need for a central authority and our need to trust that authority. The decentralisation also reduces risk. Blockchains use cryptographic techniques to secure transactions, making them resistant to fraud and hacking. Each block is linked to the previous one through a secure hash, creating a tamper-proof system. And all participants in a blockchain network have access to the same information. This transparency can enhance trust among parties involved and reduce the risk of fraud. That said, who is behind the transactions is harder to verify as wallets are just a string of letters and numbers.

Once a block is added to the blockchain, it is also extremely difficult to alter the information within it. This immutability provides a high level of data integrity and because block-chain can streamline processes by removing intermediaries, reducing paperwork, and increasing the speed of transactions it has game-changing application to the real economy – including finance.

Bitcoin, introduced in 2009 by an unknown person or group using the pseudonym Satoshi Nakamoto, was the first successful implementation of blockchain technology. Since then, numerous blockchain projects and cryptocurrencies have emerged, each with their own features and use cases. One of those features on the Ethereum blockchain is the emergence of smart contracts. Smart contracts are self-executing contracts where the terms of the agreement are written directly into the code and they therefore automatically enforce and execute the terms of such agreement when predefined conditions are met. These innovations have the potential to disrupt various industries by providing a decentralised and tamper-resistant way to record and verify transactions.

In his seminal essay *The Law of Accelerating Returns*, US inventor and futurist Ray Kurzweil states: *There's even exponential growth in the rate of exponential growth. Within a few decades, machine intelligence will surpass human intelligence, leading to The Singularity — technological change so rapid and profound it represents a rupture in the fabric of human history.*

We are fast approaching Singularity.

Chapter 4:
The Evolution of Digital Lending

Although lending has been around for thousands of years, borrowing money was an analogue, largely face-to-face, process. The party lending the money would assess the party wanting the money to decide if they were creditworthy or not.

With the advent and advance of computers and later the internet, many of the analogue processes, including the assessment of creditworthiness, were digitised and made accessible online. This included an online application process, automated underwriting, electronic documentation and digital disbursement of funds. Digital lending streamlined the lending process a little, made it more convenient for customers and was widely adopted by traditional banks. It was not particularly clever nor innovative; it simply converted analogue systems and processes onto the computer and made them more accessible to customers via the internet.

However, new non-banking players could see potential in digital lending that went beyond the digitisation of traditional services into the realm of fintech. The first such innovation was almost certainly peer-to-peer (P2P) lending, where individuals and corporations would borrow from and lend to each other. Ironically, peer-to-peer lending is how people borrowed money for centuries, long before the banks monopolised the credit market.

Written accounts of lending systems in 18th-century France, for example, document local non-notarised credit markets in small towns and villages. Locals would borrow from each other to cover shortfalls or to invest in livestock or buy seeds to plant. Everyone knew each other, built up a picture of creditworthiness over time and that was shared around the village. Those with extra money would let it be known and would lend to someone in need to help everyone prosper. And similar peer-to-peer and crowdfunding schemes could be found all over Europe, from German credit cooperatives to Irish loan funds[*].

But it was the technological advance of the early 21st century that gave this ancient lending system a modern twist. In 2005, Zopa was launched in the UK and it heralded the emergence of modern peer-to-peer lending. In an interview, co-founder David Nicholson discussed how the idea for Zopa came about . . .

One of the things I started thinking about . . . [was] what's a bank for, what does a bank really do and therefore what opportunities are there to think about how that could change . . . Obviously, banks do a huge number of things, but for a retail bank, a lot of it's quite simple. It's about matching up deposits with loans and acting as an intermediary, between somebody with a deposit and somebody with a loan . . . But what if there are other places that could act as that intermediary? Why does

---

[*] Bednorz, J., 'The History of Peer-to-Peer Lending', P2PMarketData (2023).

it have to be a bank that sits in-between depositors and people who are borrowing money?[*]

Instead of imagining the future, Nicholson looked to the past and realised that there were, 'some pretty simple basic building blocks underneath [the banking system]'. In other words, he suggested that if you looked back one or two hundred years, no one except banks had any of the information, systems, or technology to allow them to take on the role of that intermediary function[†]. But the emergence of digital lending potentially changed all that.

It's also no accident that, before launching Zopa, the three founders, Nicholson, Richard Duval and James Alexander, worked for Egg, an online bank created by Prudential in 1998. Egg was the first company in the UK to introduce end-to-end online applications for credit cards. Its early commercial success also demonstrated that customers were happy to interact exclusively online. This realisation, together with his musings about banking, led to Zopa. Nicholson believed that banks were essentially the union of 'two markets': a borrowers' market (loans) and a lenders' market (deposits). And he believed that too many people in the borrowers' market, such as contract workers, were not getting credit because they didn't tick the right boxes. In the lenders' market, Nicholson believed Zopa could win over those who wanted some real connection to where their money would end up and the savvy financiers who would use P2P loans as a new asset class and to diversify their portfolios.

---

[*] Atz, U. and Bholat, D., 'Peer-to-peer lending and financial innovation in the United Kingdom', Staff Working Paper No. 598, Bank of England (2016).

[†] Ibid.

Ironically, the biggest hurdle that Zopa and the other P2P lenders that followed, including Lending Club and Prosper, needed to deal with was their own credibility or creditworthiness. In the beginning, P2P lending was considered 'niche' at best and 'shady' at worst.

The turning point for P2P lending was the GFC. Prior to the GFC, the banks were held in high regard and public confidence was high, and that made P2P lending a challenging sell. After the GFC, when the actions and behaviours of traditional banks were laid bare, public confidence collapsed along with the traditional lines of credit from those banks. As banks basically closed the doors to vast swaths of borrowers, including SMEs, it was initially P2P lending providers who stepped into the gap. And alternative funding and even more fintech companies have flooded into that gap ever since.

Today, P2P lending is present in most parts of the world and has diversified with many platforms specialising in certain types of loans. No longer considered niche or shady, P2P lending is an intrinsic part of the financial system. And it was the first example of fintech lending, a subset of digital lending. Instead of just digitising information and providing online access to customers, fintech companies, often start-ups and non-traditional financial institutions, use technology to innovate and disrupt traditional lending models. And that's exactly what P2P lending did – these offerings by non-banks inserted themselves digitally between the two markets of borrowers and lenders and used advanced algorithms, data analytics and digital platforms to offer a more efficient, user-friendly, and often faster lending solution.

Unfortunately, the P2P model also had some limitations that prevented it from becoming the clear contender to replace or supplement the role of banks in lending markets. One of the key challenges for P2P businesses is the acquisition of users. We now have more than two decades of experience in analysing web-based consumer businesses: low barriers to entry led to increased competition, which led to a race to acquire clients. It is therefore not surprising that companies such as Google or Meta, the advertising gateways to the eyeballs of billions of online users, became trillion-dollar companies*. The outcome of this process is a constant trend towards an increased Customer Acquisition Cost (CAC), with web-based consumer businesses often having to spend 20 to 30 per cent of their revenues on marketing on a regular basis. The problem with the P2P model is that, being a marketplace, the customer acquisition needs are double: they need to attract both borrowers and lenders! Consequently, very few P2P players managed to reach adequate scale due to the lack of resources to feed the marketing needs.

The second challenge is even more difficult to tackle. Banks receive deposits and lend money. However, Central Banks act as a circuit breaker by guaranteeing deposits up to a certain amount. In times of crisis, banks can still rely on deposits because depositors feel protected by such guarantees. P2P, on the other end, rarely offers protection and the limited protection it can offer does not provide the same comfort as a Central Bank. That makes the supply of capital in a P2P network highly volatile, with investors often fleeing the market at the time when capital is most required. Over the years, P2P players reacted by including institutional capital in their funding base, but, on its own, this solution is not

---

* 'List of public corporations by market capitalization', Wikipedia, [accessed January 2024].

enough to solve the problem. These challenges and the limits of the P2P model contributed to a rapid evolution of ideas that constitute the beginning of the fintech revolution.

The key to understanding the explosive evolution of fintech is to appreciate technologies and processes that are levelling the financial services playing field with traditional banking. There are four building blocks that have facilitated this exponential growth:

1. Big Data and Open Banking;
2. Artificial Intelligence (AI);
3. Process Automation;
4. A Network Approach.

Big Data and Open Banking

Big data refers to extremely large and complex datasets that can be analysed to extract meaning, find patterns and make predictions. If the datasets are large enough, correlations can be made that indicate probability, and it is these insights that are changing the face of finance and leaving traditional banks struggling to keep up.

As mentioned in the last chapter, we live in a datafied and digitised world, where all sorts of different data points and types of data are easier to track and collect than ever before. But collecting or having the data is just part of the puzzle. Traditional banks have mountains of data, often going back decades. But this data is contained in legacy systems, held in different departments and those departments don't necessarily share data or talk to each other. In some cases, the data may still be on microfiche or in paper archives. As such, it is incredibly challenging, time-consuming and costly for traditional banks to utilise the vast amount of data they have and they are therefore at a significant disadvantage to fintech companies designed with big data in mind from the start. To borrow an analogy from the previous chapter, fintech leapfrogged banks in big data in a similar fashion to how emerging markets leapfrogged developed markets on telecommunication technology.

> We live in a datafied and digitised world, where all sorts of different data points and types of data are easier to track and collect than ever before.

Although traditional banks recognise the issue they face and many are trying to change the infrastructure to accommodate more sharing and make better use of the data, this is undoubtedly a challenging and a very expensive task. Using big data effectively is also a mindset issue, and many in traditional banking are still locked into that legacy mindset and find it difficult to step outside that mindset to see what's possible.

Big data is usually characterised by 5Vs.

- **Volume:** Big data involves massive amounts of data. This could be terabytes, petabytes or even larger datasets. The sheer volume is a key characteristic of big data.
- **Velocity:** Big data is generated and collected at high speed. Data streams in rapidly, often in real time, from various sources such as social media, sensors, clickstreams, and more. The velocity of data flow distinguishes big data from traditional datasets.

- **Variety:** Big data comes in various formats. It includes structured data (like databases), unstructured data (like text and images) and semi-structured data (like JSON or XML files). The diversity of data types adds complexity to big data analysis.
- **Variability:** This refers to the inconsistency that can be present in the data. Data might be inconsistent due to discrepancies in data sources, data quality issues or other factors.
- **Veracity:** Veracity refers to the reliability and trustworthiness of the data. In big data scenarios, there can be concerns about the accuracy of data, and ensuring data quality becomes a challenge.

Big data analytics aims to uncover hidden patterns, correlations, and other valuable information from large datasets to deliver a better outcome and a competitive advantage. Take credit risk as an example. The first known credit reporting occurred in 1803 in England when a group of tailors came together to swap information about customers who failed to settle their debts. In 1826 the Manchester Guardian Society formed to issue a monthly newsletter with information about people who failed to pay their debts. In 1864 in New York, R.G. Dun and Company, formerly the Mercantile Agency, established a numerical system for tracking the creditworthiness of companies. This system was the benchmark well into the 20th century. By the mid-1950s, US consumers were rotating several credit cards. The need to track their creditworthiness grew and early credit reporters used millions of index cards to keep track of consumers' buying and repaying behaviour.

By 1964, the Association of Credit Bureaus in the US conducted the first studies into the application of the new computer technology on credit reporting. Even then, it was easy to see that computers had the potential to improve credit assessment and reduce risk[*].

In 1989 the FICO score was introduced in the US and quickly became the standard system for measuring credit scores based on objective factors and data. FICO – named after the company who introduced it, the Fair Isaac Corporation – allocated a credit score based on:

- Payment history (35%);
- Amounts owed (30%);
- New credit (10%);
- Length of credit history (15%);
- Credit mix (10%).

Ninety out of 100 institutions in the US still use FICO to assess credit risk. But big data is changing all that. Instead of viewing a snapshot of credit data at a moment in time, the use of trend data makes it possible to track creditworthiness in real time. This alone is delivering a 20 per cent improvement in predictive performance against the traditional FICO static credit assessments[†].

In addition, the use of alternative data is yielding genuinely surprising results. The importance of alternative data is particularly evident in those scenarios where risk underwriting needs to happen in real time, as with a typical

---

[*] Desjardins, J., 'The History of Consumer Credit in One Giant Infographic', Visual Capitalist (2017).

[†] Ibid.

fintech product such as 'buy-now-pay-later' (BNPL). This product allows a customer executing a purchase on an ecommerce website to split the payment over a few instalments. Clearly, such product requires an assessment of the probability of repayment from that specific customer, but the assessment needs to happen in real time in order to avoid the outcome most feared by any ecommerce player: cart abandonment. It is this real time underwriting need that forces fintech companies to use as much alternative information as possible. For example, a European BNPL company requires the input of the National Tax Code at time of sign-up before approving a transaction. Most people know their code by heart as they use it regularly in their daily lives. The company tracks how long it takes a user to input the Tax Code and whether the use of the backspace button took place while typing it. Over tens of thousands of sign-ups and transactions, the company was able to assess the correlation between fraud and the time required to input the code. The logic is simple: there is a higher probability that the attempt is fraudulent when the user takes too long or uses the backspace button because they are more likely to be using a fake code. Note that this is just a higher probability. The two items being tracked, *time to input the Tax Code* and *use of backspace button while inputting the Tax Code*, simply represent data points that, with a certain weighting, will be used in a complex algorithm to assess the *probability* of fraud. These alternative data points are impossible to collect in an analogue world, unless every client is hooked up to a polygraph test while they are filling in the application form. The same BNPL company processes many thousands of transactions per day, spread across the whole country. If three sign-ups happen within ten minutes of each other for purchases of the maximum amount allowed with three different users at the same address, the system knows from past experience that this is highly unusual and the only similar cases in the past have led to fraud. As a result, the transaction is rejected.

Once again, the analysis of data from the past and simple probability calculations allow the company to assess more accurately the chance of fraud based on user behaviour.

This company, like so many in the fintech space, is delivering a service with zero visibility upfront. So, it needs to consider all the different hints or clues that a customer provides in the signing-up stage to figure out if something might be wrong. If a potential customer thinks, 'This is great, I'll sign up for three accounts and get three sets of immediate credit,' the system is ready.

This is not possible in the traditional banking system. A loan application could be made at two different branches and it may not be discovered for weeks, if at all. Banks certainly couldn't collect data on how quickly someone enters information on a form, never mind think outside the box to interpret what it might mean. In legacy banking systems, applications are often pre-completed by the people paid the least whereas highly paid and highly qualified Data Scientists at the very top of a fintech company are thinking about all the different angles, additional datasets and innovative analytics that can be used to improve checks and reduce fraud – in real time.

Big data advances have, of course, gone hand in glove with cloud computing capability. Cloud computing has allowed fintech companies access to vast amounts of data, different types of data, a way for that data to be stored effectively and economically, ways to search and manipulate that data to yield connections, patterns and predictions that are then used to deliver a better service to customers.

But it is not just the data collected on a specific user at the time of sign-up that gets used for assessment. Nowadays, even what is posted on social media can give hints and suggestions and help categorise clients based on their behaviours. If your LinkedIn shows that you have an entry-level sales job at a clothing store and your Facebook posts show you regularly holiday abroad, there is a possibility that your saving rate may be low. Once again, we are talking about *possibility* and ensuing probabilities. Big data is about finding a smart way to give the appropriate weighting to any available data point used in making a judgement call. That is very different from face-to-face banking, where information bias of a decision-maker can easily lead to suboptimal decisions.

Levelling the playing field between traditional banks and fintech lending platforms has been further facilitated by 'Open Banking', both directly through regulation and access and indirectly by allowing for even larger datasets.

> Levelling the playing field between traditional banks and fintech lending platforms has been further facilitated by 'Open Banking'.

Open Banking refers to a system where banks open their Application Programming Interfaces (APIs) to third-party developers. This system enables the secure sharing of financial information, typically with the consent of the customer, for the purpose of creating new apps and services. It allows fintech companies access to banking data, thus encouraging innovation in the financial services industry. Fintechs, which are usually more agile and creative than traditional banks, can develop personalised financial products and services. This competition pushes traditional banks to innovate as well, leading to a more dynamic market.

It also means improved financial inclusion with fintechs able to use Open Banking to access a customer's financial history from various banks. This comprehensive view enables them to offer credit and other financial products to individuals and small businesses that might be underserved by traditional banks.

Open Banking democratises access to financial data, fostering a more competitive and innovative environment in the financial services sector. It enables fintech companies to offer more tailored and accessible services, benefiting consumers and small businesses while also enhancing the overall financial market's efficiency and transparency.

The first major implementation of Open Banking can be traced back to the United Kingdom. The UK's Open Banking journey began with a regulatory initiative, primarily driven by two key developments:

- **European Union's PSD2 Directive:** The Payment Services Directive 2 (PSD2), issued by the European Union, was a significant regulatory mandate that played a pivotal role in the development of Open Banking. Introduced in 2015 and implemented in 2018, PSD2 required banks to provide third-party providers (TPPs) access to their customers' accounts (with the customer's consent) to enable the development of new financial services. While PSD2 was a Europe-wide directive, its adoption and impact were particularly notable in the UK.

- **Competition and Markets Authority (CMA) Order:** In the UK specifically, the move towards Open Banking was accelerated by the Competition and Markets Authority (CMA). In 2016, the CMA ordered the nine biggest banks in the UK to allow licensed start-ups direct access to their data, down to the level of transactional account data. This order was a part of a broader effort to increase competition and innovation in the banking sector.

These regulatory actions laid the groundwork for Open Banking in the UK, setting a precedent that has been followed by various other countries globally. The UK's model of Open Banking is often cited as a leading example of how regulatory initiatives can drive innovation in the financial sector, benefiting consumers through increased competition and the availability of new financial products and services. It is, however, worth pointing out that, whilst the UK model represents a success, many other jurisdictions have been slower to adopt Open Banking, as banks try to interfere with measures that they believe would weaken their grip on the market[*]. This is a mistake, similar to the mistake the record industry made when seeking to stop music sharing sites like Napster in 2001. They didn't appreciate that the market wanted to access music differently. Banks slow to adopt Open Banking are making the same mistake by not appreciating that their customers want something different and better. Change is here and Open Banking gives banks

---

[*]   Guilhon, M., 'Limitations to open banking regulations in Europe', *The Banker* (2022).

a real opportunity to innovate alongside fintech and stay relevant.

Artificial Intelligence (AI)

The concept of AI can be traced back to the 1940s and 1950s. In his 1950 paper titled *Computing Machinery and Intelligence*, mathematician and computer scientist, Alan Turing, proposed the Turing Test, a benchmark for determining a machine's ability to exhibit intelligent behaviour indistinguishable from that of a human.

The test involves a human judge who engages in natural language conversations with both a human and a machine without knowing which is which. If the judge cannot reliably distinguish between the human and the machine based on the conversation alone, then the machine is said to have passed the Turing Test.

Although the Turing Test faced criticisms, with some commentators arguing that it set a low bar for intelligence, it was still a landmark moment – proof that a machine could function like a human in certain limited circumstances. The outcome of that innovation is seen today in chatbots for example, that can help customers in very limited, scripted ways. Although they are not yet demonstrating true general intelligence, their function does serve a purpose in modern customer service.

While no machine has definitively passed the Turing Test in all aspects, there have been instances where judges were unable to consistently distinguish between human and machine responses during specific interactions. Today, this is certainly true of ChatGPT, the new kid on the AI block.

The Turing Test remains a thought-provoking concept in

the field of artificial intelligence and philosophy, stimulating discussions about the nature of intelligence and the potential for machines to achieve human-like cognitive abilities.

Between the 1950s and 1960s, early AI research focused on rule-based systems and problem-solving. For example, Allen Newell, Cliff Shaw and Herbert Simon's, Logic Theorist was a program designed to mimic the problem-solving skills of a human. Funded by Research and Development (RAND), Logic Theorist is considered by many to be the first artificial intelligence program and it was presented at the Dartmouth Summer Research Project on Artificial Intelligence (DSRPAI) hosted by John McCarthy and Marvin Minsky in 1956. The term *artificial intelligence* was coined at this historic conference, considered the birthplace of AI as a field of study[*].

Early demonstrations, such as Newell and Simon's General Problem Solver in 1959, showed additional promise toward the goals of problem-solving. Research during the 1960s and 1970s emphasised symbolic AI, where computers manipulated symbols and logic to simulate human reasoning. Expert systems, which used knowledge from human specialists to solve specific problems, gained in popularity.

But the initial frenzy about machines that could replicate human intelligence never quite delivered on the promise and the 1980s saw a period known as the 'AI winter', where unmet expectations reduced funding and interest. That frenzy, however, clearly inspired scriptwriters and in 1984 the movie *Terminator* was released. Directed by James

---

[*] Anyoha, R., *The History of Artificial Intelligence* (Harvard University, 2017).

Cameron and starring Arnold Schwarzenegger, it depicted a cyborg assassin back from 2029 when AI had become more intelligent than human beings and had taken over the world. This dystopian fear of AI has been bubbling away ever since. In 2023 several AI experts, including CEOs, policy-makers and scientists signed an open letter calling attention to the existential risk AI posed to the human race[*]. Clearly something had happened in the interim to warrant that concern.

In the late 1990s, AI science and research experienced a resurgence, with advancements in machine learning, neural networks and the development of more powerful computers making a huge difference. Machine learning (ML) is a subset of AI that focuses on the development of algorithms and statistical models that enable computers to improve their performance on a specific task over time through experience. In other words, instead of being explicitly programmed to perform a task, a machine learning system learns from data and examples, allowing it to generalise and make predictions or decisions without being explicitly programmed for each scenario. There are several types of ML approaches including:

- **Supervised learning:** The algorithm is trained on a labelled dataset, where the correct outputs are provided. It learns to map inputs to corresponding outputs.
- **Unsupervised learning:** The algorithm is given unlabelled data and must find patterns or relationships within the data without explicit guidance.

---

[*] Vallance, C., 'Artificial intelligence could lead to extinction, experts warn', BBC News (2023).

- **Reinforcement learning:** The algorithm learns by interacting with an environment and receiving feedback in the form of rewards or penalties. It aims to learn a sequence of actions that maximise cumulative reward.
- **Semi-Supervised learning:** This approach combines labelled and unlabelled data for training, often useful when obtaining labelled data is costly or time-consuming.
- **Deep learning:** Deep learning is a subset of machine learning that involves neural networks with many layers (deep neural networks). It has shown remarkable success in tasks such as image and speech recognition.

Machine learning, neural networks, and deep learning can be applied to various domains, including natural language processing, image and speech recognition and recommendation systems. Tasks include classification, regression, pattern recognition and feature extraction. These tools are incredibly flexible and can adapt to different types of data making them powerful tools for solving complex problems. The architecture and complexity of neural networks can vary from simple models to complex structures with millions of parameters. They have become a foundational technology in AI, powering many state-of-the-art applications.

The first widely publicised demonstration of the power of machine learning was in 1997, when IBM's Deep Blue defeated world chess champion Garry Kasparov in a historic match. Chess is a game of strategy, and being able to anticipate several moves ahead. The idea that a machine could accomplish this faster and see further was disconcerting to many. The same year, spoken language recognition and interpretation took another step forward when speech recognition software, developed by Dragon Systems, was implemented on Windows. Kismet, developed by Dr Cynthia Breazeal at the Massachusetts Institute of Technology (MIT), looked a little like a robotic gremlin but it could recognise and display human emotions.

> The first widely publicised demonstration of the power of machine learning was in 1997 when IBM's Deep Blue defeated world chess champion Garry Kasparov.

The 2000s marked significant advance in machine learning, with the development of support vector machines (SVM), decision trees and ensemble learning techniques. SVM and decision trees are both supervised machine learning algorithms used for classification and regression tasks. Ensemble learning techniques are machine learning techniques that involve combining the predictions of multiple models to improve overall performance, accuracy and robustness. Ensemble methods aim to overcome the limitations of individual models by leveraging the strengths of a group of models. The idea is that the collective wisdom of multiple models can often lead to better results than any single model on its own. Data-driven approaches certainly gained prominence in the 2000s, in large part because of the corresponding advance in big data and cloud computing that allowed for the storage and analysis of extremely large datasets.

It's not so much that our ability to create AI has become so much better; it's just that the fundamental limit of computer storage and computational power was holding us back. In 1965, Gordon Moore, co-founder of Intel Corporation, observed that the number of transistors on a dense integrated circuit (IC) was doubling approximately every two years. This may explain why AI development has been such a rollercoaster; capabilities eventually hit a ceiling in current computational power and must wait for Moore's Law to catch up[*].

With the advent of cloud computing, there may no longer be a ceiling – hence the existential threat fears!

The 2010s was the decade of deep learning: a subset of machine learning, using neural networks with many layers (deep neural networks) and led to breakthroughs in image and speech recognition. Once again, the success of deep learning was exemplified to the public through a game. This time by projects like Google's DeepMind, which developed AlphaGo, an AI that defeated eight-time world champion Go player, Lee Sedol, in 2016. To get a sense of the magnitude of this achievement, it's worth unpacking the win. Although Go has simple rules, its complexity is staggering. After just three pairs of moves in chess there are about 121 million possible configurations of the board. But after three moves in Go, there are around 200 quadrillion possible configurations. When Deep Blue beat Kasparov in 1997, it used a method called 'brute force', essentially systematically crunching through many possible moves until it won. But the computational possibilities of Go mean 'brute force' doesn't work. There are more configurations of a Go board than there are atoms in the known universe. Instead, AlphaGo learned, initially at least, by watching 150,000 games played

---

[*]   Anyoha, R., *The History of Artificial Intelligence* (Harvard University, 2017).

by human experts. Once some competence was generated via this method, lots of copies of AlphaGo were created so the system could play against itself over and over again and develop new strategies that it had never even seen. On the day of the tournament, AlphaGo won the first game. In the second game AlphaGo made what commentators at the time described as a 'very strange move'. It was so unusual that Sedol took fifteen minutes to respond and even went outside for a walk. Although everyone thought AlphaGo had made a huge mistake, it eventually won again. What is so stunning about the win is that AlphaGo rewrote Go strategy and utilised a move that hadn't been considered by the most brilliant Go players over thousands of years. AlphaGo beat Sedol 4-1 and later versions of the software like AlphaZero have dispensed with human knowledge altogether and simply train on their own, playing itself millions of times, learning new and novel ways to win that have never been deployed. AlphaZero was capable of learning more about the game of Go in one day than was known about Go across the entirety of human experience. And AlphaGo's win heralded a new age of AI[*].

Today, AI technologies are increasingly integrated into various aspects of daily life, including fintech. As a field of study, it has been characterised by cycles of optimism followed by periods of scepticism but it always rebounds, with each cycle contributing to the overall progress and understanding of artificial intelligence.

---

[*] Sulleyman, M. and Bhasker, M., *The Coming Wave* (Vintage, London, 2023).

Today, AI technologies are increasingly integrated into
various aspects of daily life, including fintech.

There is also a constant push from institutional investors
who are often behind fintech companies. There is a clear
correlation between the value of a company and its utilisation
of technology, including AI. In short, fintech companies that
utilise AI command a much bigger valuation and there is
often a more exciting and engaging story to tell as a result.

This is in stark contrast to the traditional banking sector.
Although AI is being used in the traditional banking sector, given that it can be applied to data anywhere, because
of the legacy mindset and legacy systems, this sector's
application of AI tends to be more inhibited than fintech's
own. Traditional banks are very used to doing certain things
a certain way and are not necessarily as open, inventive or
creative. Fintech players have these capabilities hardwired
into their DNA and know that gaining an edge is the only way
to compete with legacy businesses. It's also a systems issue.
According to McKinsey & Co, many banks are struggling
to move from experimentation around select-use cases of AI
to scaling these technologies across the organisation. This is
because of a range of issues, from the lack of a clear strategy
for AI to an inflexible and investment-starved technology
core and fragmented data assets, where the data they do have
is locked inside departmental silos. Outmoded operating
models also hamper collaboration between business and
technology teams[*].

---

[*] Biswas, S., Carson, B., Chung, V., Singh, S. and Thomas, R.,
AI-bank of the future: Can banks meet the AI challenge?,
McKinsey & Company (2020).

That said, traditional banks are seeking to embrace AI and incorporate it into their existing processes to personalise services to customers, reduce costs through efficiencies generated by high automation and uncovering new and previously unrealised opportunities based on an improved ability to process and generate insights from their data. McKinsey estimates that AI technologies could potentially deliver up to $1 trillion of additional value each year to global banking[*].

Whereas the most used AI technologies in banking are Robotic Process Automation (RPA) used for structured operational tasks and virtual assistants or chatbots, AI is already being used to enhance efficiency, improve customer experiences and make more informed decisions inside most fintech companies.

The AI capabilities include:

- **Credit scoring and risk assessment:** AI algorithms analyse vast amounts of information and enrich datasets with alternative data to assess the creditworthiness of individuals and businesses. Models are constantly refined and recalibrated with the inclusion of new sources of information as soon as they become available. Performance of the model is tracked in real time to assess the need to change direction.
- **Fraud detection and prevention:** AI is used to detect and prevent fraudulent activities in real time. Machine learning algorithms analyse patterns and anomalies

---

[*] Biswas, S., Carson, B., Chung, V., Singh, S. and Thomas, R., *AI-bank of the future: Can banks meet the AI challenge?*, McKinsey & Company (2020).

in transactions to identify potentially fraudulent behaviour and trigger alerts for further investigation. As we have seen in the examples presented earlier in this chapter, the more data we have, the more opportunities to discover interesting patterns and correlations that could lead to more accurate predictions.

- **Chatbots and virtual assistants:** AI-powered chatbots and virtual assistants provide instant customer support, answer queries and assist with tasks such as account inquiries, transaction history and basic financial advice. This is an area currently expanding at a rapid pace: while early chatbots were simply automated replies to easy questions, now virtual assistants can take on increasingly complex tasks, even helping marketing teams in outbound sales activities.

- **Personalised banking and financial planning:** AI algorithms analyse customer behaviour, preferences and financial history to offer personalised recommendations for banking products, investment options and financial planning strategies.

- **Algorithmic trading:** AI algorithms are employed in algorithmic trading to analyse market trends, execute trades and optimise investment portfolios. These systems can make split-second decisions based on large volumes of data.

- **Customer relationship management (CRM):** AI enhances CRM systems by analysing customer interactions and providing insights that help financial institutions tailor their services to individual needs. This leads to improved customer satisfaction and retention.

- **Regulatory compliance:** AI is used to streamline regulatory compliance processes. Automated systems can monitor and ensure that financial transactions adhere to local and international regulations, reducing the risk of non-compliance.
- **Robo-advisors:** AI-driven robo-advisors provide automated, algorithm-based financial planning services. They analyse customer risk tolerance, investment goals and market conditions to recommend and manage investment portfolios.
- **Natural language processing (NLP):** NLP allows financial institutions to analyse and understand unstructured data, such as news articles, social media and customer feedback, to gain insights into market sentiment and potential risks.

There is certainly more scope for traditional banks to catch up with fintech around the building block of AI as opposed to big data. Unlike the capability of big data, which would require expensive and time-consuming infrastructure and system change, AI can be utilised more effectively by empowering a small team of people with the ability to access the data the bank holds and figure out the connections and make recommendations for innovations and process improvements that may indeed deliver that trillion-dollar boost McKinsey envisages. Their biggest hurdle will be their mindset and how to become 'AI-First' institutions and finding ways to roll out the initiatives safely. There is, however, little doubt that the AI building block at least will not remain a source of competitive advantage for fintechs for much longer.

Process Automation

The third building block behind the explosion of fintech is process automation. This comes from development of the internet and the advance of high-speed broadband. First, the internet gave us the opportunity to massively reduce the time it took to do various tasks. Before the internet we had to physically travel to a location or call someone to shop, book a holiday, buy insurance, take care of our banking needs or action any number of activities we needed to get done. Then the internet came along and a huge proportion of these processes and functions moved online. Granted, initially they were not that exciting and dial-up internet meant that most people carried on going to the shops or visiting the local travel agent. The alternative was not good enough to warrant the switch.

But broadband arrived in the early 2000s and changed everything. In the previous decade the internet did improve. Websites looked better and offered a far faster, cheaper service. Search capability revolutionised several time-consuming and boring processes like sourcing the best current account, buying home insurance or finding a car.

The iPhone arrived in 2007 making the internet mobile for the first time. Users were no longer limited to internet access on a desktop computer in their spare bedroom; they could jump online via a browser on their phone or gain access to products and services via apps that made it even easier to order everything from their weekly shopping to an Uber.

The evolution of mobile applications, commonly known as apps, has been dynamic and transformative since the introduction of the first mobile phones. The early phones of the 1990s were just phones. Later we could send SMS messages and there were basic applications, often built into the phone's firmware, such as a calculator, calendars and address book. In the 2000s Java Micro Edition (Java ME) emerged as a platform for mobile application development. It allowed developers to create more sophisticated applications for feature phones, expanding beyond basic utilities. And in 2008, a year after the launch of the iPhone, Apple introduced the App Store which proved to be a transformative moment. The App Store provided a centralised platform for users to discover, download and install third-party applications, and the concept of an app store was quickly adopted by other platforms.

The iPhone and Android devices took off, bringing more powerful hardware and advanced operating systems. This enabled the development of feature-rich and visually appealing apps. And the app ecosystem expanded rapidly in the 2010s with a diverse range of apps catering to various needs, including social media, productivity, entertainment and more, all, incidentally, creating even more data for the corresponding big data, analytics and AI revolutions. Social media alone is an astonishingly vast data pool, although changes to privacy rules have made it far harder to access. For example, Apple's iOS 14.5 operating system update in 2021, which required users to explicitly opt-in to allow companies to collect their data, cost Facebook $10 billion in advertising revenue*. But in the 2010s both the Apple App Store and Google Play Store saw exponential growth in the number of available apps.

---

* Naughton, J., 'For the first time in its history, Facebook is in decline. Has the tech giant begun to crumble?', *Guardian* (2022).

Developers began adopting cross-platform frameworks, such as React Native and Xamarin, to create apps that could run on multiple platforms. This helped streamline the development process and reach a broader audience. Apps also started incorporating Augmented Reality (AR) and Virtual Reality (VR) technologies for enhanced user experiences. Games, education and retail apps began leveraging AR to provide interactive and immersive content.

Progressive web apps emerged as a new approach to app development, offering a blend of web and native app features. PWAs allow users to access app-like experiences directly through web browsers without the need for traditional app installations. This innovation itself is another nod to process automation, where users can access app functionality without the additional step of downloading the app!

The evolution of apps has closely followed the advancements in mobile technology, from basic utilities on feature phones to the sophisticated and diverse range of applications available on today's smartphones and other connected devices. Apps are becoming more personalised, intelligent and seamlessly integrated into users' daily lives and our expectation of their functionality is constantly rising.

During this evolution, tech companies in fintech and elsewhere have become obsessed with process automation and how they can remove as many steps as possible to reduce friction and increase conversion rates. We know this ourselves instinctively. How many times have we agreed to take an online survey because it starts with one question, only to give up after the fifth question? Or when we have decided to buy a product from an online store only to have second thoughts when the checkout process is too long or complex? Once again, being 'web-first' or 'mobile-first', and having to rely on smaller teams, made fintech players more driven than traditional banks to leverage process automation.

We live in a world obsessed with immediate gratification. Our 24/7 access to the internet via our mobile phone has certainly fuelled that obsession. We want to be able to decide something and action it in seconds, not minutes – *seconds*. We expect this and we have been trained to expect this by providers who have sought to achieve greater and greater process automations.

There are now people whose entire role is based on figuring out how to set up a website and where to put the buy button to increase conversation and remove as many unnecessary steps as possible. The undisputed king of process automation in fintech is of course Amazon, with its one-click checkout intuition. What makes it a brilliant innovation is the fact that it was patented in 1997, when ecommerce was a tiny industry; websites were still very basic and most people went online through dial-in modems. If we include payment services in the broader fintech category, we could probably consider this one of the first great fintech innovations. So great that even the mighty Apple (at that time not yet so mighty) decided to license the technology in 2000. People browse the site and can click on *buy* once and the process is fully automated; the user gets an order confirmation email in seconds and the product arrives the next day. Everything works smoothly because Amazon has stored all the information required at the first purchase. It feels psychologically satisfying to the buyer and it maintains sky-high conversion rates for the platform.

Process automation is a critical competitive advantage for fintech companies because they don't have to work around legacy systems and are able to design the systems with speed and efficiency in mind. Revolut and other neobanks, for example, have gone to great lengths to reduce the number of steps to open an account and obtain a new bank card. It is a game of numbers: every step eliminated represents an increase in sign-ups and entire teams are dedicated to optimise the process.

Process automation is a critical competitive advantage for fintech companies because they don't have to work around legacy systems.

This obsession with process automation doesn't just benefit the customer with faster delivery of the product or service. Because these processes are automated, they represent an insignificant marginal cost for a fintech. A would-be customer at Revolut is not, for example, visiting a bricks-and-mortar branch with all its running costs and is not speaking to a customer services staff member whose salary needs to be paid. The account can be opened very quickly at a very low cost, which in turn allows Revolut to provide services to areas of the market that could not be reached in the past because they were unprofitable to serve. This is true of all fintech companies: the automation of technology makes it possible to make money in new ways from new markets while serving an unmet need.

Picture the most successful bank branch: clients come in to be served and, based on the number of employees, a relatively small number of customers gets onboarded. Now contrast it with a mobile app: a successful neobank can sign up as many clients as there are. If too many arrive at the same time, cloud computing solves the problem by borrowing storage and processing capacity and immediately scales to meet the need. This level of process automation is transformational.

A Network Approach

At its core, Web 1.0, the first version of the internet, was the creation of an information exchange system. Various protocols such as the Internet Protocol (IP), File Transfer Protocol, Simple Mail Transfer Protocol (SMTP) and many others allowed for information to be shared and exchanged far faster than was possible in the off-line world.

Even before the internet, part of the challenge in computing was how to get various systems to talk to each other. The concept of Application Programming Interfaces (APIs) has therefore been a fundamental part of software development for many years. Like most critical aspects of technology, their creation, development and refinement has been an open-source, collaborative effort driven by the need for software systems to communicate and interact with each other.

Even in the early days of computing, developers needed ways for programs to communicate and share data. Techniques such as shared memory and inter-process communication served as early forms of APIs. With the development of operating systems, APIs became a means for applications to interact with the underlying operating system. Operating system APIs provided a standardised way for software to access system resources and services.

The rise of the internet and the World Wide Web brought about a new era for APIs. Web APIs became crucial for enabling communication between web servers and clients. Technologies like SOAP (Simple Object Access Protocol) and later REST (Representational State Transfer) played significant roles in defining web-based APIs.

In the early years of the internet, developers, from the technically trained to the hobbyist in their bedroom, were in their element, coming up with new ideas, programs and ways to use the internet. Unsurprisingly, there was very little standardisation. There were no rules on how these innovations were being developed. The result was a bunch of protocols and innovations that may have been brilliant in their own sandbox or closed system but that couldn't then connect or communicate to anything else.

For the internet to deliver on its potential this needed to change. Organisations, such as the World Wide Web Consortium (W3C), the Internet Engineering Task Force (IETF) and others contributed to the standardisation of web-related technologies, including protocols and formats used in APIs.

This was transformative because it allowed for the creation of genuine networks, where APIs, essentially types of software interfaces, were able to offer a service to other pieces of software. The rise in the popularity of social media platforms from the mid-2000s onwards led to the development of APIs that allowed developers to integrate their applications with services like Twitter, Facebook and others. These APIs opened new possibilities for third-party app development.

While the concept of APIs has been around for a long time, the modern understanding of APIs, especially in the context of web development and services, has evolved over the past few decades. Today, APIs are integral to software development, enabling interoperability, integration and the creation of complex and interconnected systems. APIs have also been instrumental in creating what is known as the network effect.

> Today, APIs are integral to software development, enabling interoperability, integration and the creation of complex and interconnected systems.

The network effect is a phenomenon in which the value of a product or service increases as more people use it. In other words, the more users a network has (often facilitated by APIs), the more valuable it becomes to each individual user. We can see this in everything from fax machines to the internet to social media. When only one person had a fax machine it wasn't much use. But once there was a fax machine in every office in the world it was an extremely useful business tool. Once email came along, the fax died out. But email was only useful when everyone had an email address. The internet only became an embedded part of our life when billions of people were connected to it. And it's not much fun having a social media profile if you have three friends!

The network effect was first noticed by Bob Metcalfe, the co-inventor of Ethernet in 1990 when he created 'Metcalfe's Law'. Metcalfe's Law states that the value of a communication network is proportional to the square of the number of connected users of the system[*]. In other words, every time you add a new participant to the network, you don't just slightly increase the effectiveness of the network, you square the effectiveness of the whole network.

As more people use a product or service, made more possible or improved by APIs, each user derives more value from it. This increased value can result from factors like enhanced communication, more available content or a larger user base for network-based services. The growing network therefore creates a positive feedback loop where

---

[*]   Naughton, J., 'For the first time in its history, Facebook is in decline. Has the tech giant begun to crumble?', *Guardian* (2022).

the network effect creates a self-reinforcing cycle. As more users join, the product becomes more valuable, attracting even more users. And this positive feedback loop contributes to rapid growth.

The value increases for users directly participating in the network, such as in social media platforms or communication apps. Or the value increases for users as more complementary products or services become available (because of APIs). For example, the value of a gaming console increases as more games are developed for it. Or the value increases for users on two sides of a platform. For instance, in a marketplace, more buyers attract more sellers and vice versa – this is something we are already seeing as finance becomes more and more embedded.

When a business or platform creates a network effect it becomes a significant barrier to entry for new competitors. Established networks with a large user base are often more attractive to users than new or smaller networks.

It was APIs that allowed the network effect to expand beyond closed systems and they have been transformational in fintech. For centuries, banks have been closed systems, they have guarded their data and IP fiercely. But that mindset is now a hindrance that fintech just doesn't have. Add changing regulation around Open Banking and closed systems are a thing of the past.

> It was APIs that allowed the network effect
> to expand beyond closed systems and they
> have been transformational in fintech.

APIs have allowed for the creation of vast networks that spread out far beyond a single, independent, centralised company such as a bank. Instead, there is now a network of companies, including fintechs, that do a small part of a business process in an extremely fast, efficient and accurate way.

This is very similar to what happened in the Industrial Revolution – only digitally. Part of what made the Industrial Revolution so transformative was the 'division of labour'. Coined by Scottish economist and philosopher, Adam Smith, in his seminal work *The Wealth of Nations*, it had a profound impact on economic thought and laid the groundwork for understanding the benefits of specialisation. Smith argued that dividing the production process into smaller, specialised tasks could significantly increase overall productivity. This would accumulate skill in that task and factories were built up around the idea of creating one thing and one thing only, but doing it efficiently. Such an approach also created economies of scale and extended market reach. Combined with steam-powered mechanisation, automation, greater transport links and urbanisation these marked a transformative period in history characterised by significant economic, technological and social changes.

APIs are doing the same in the digital world of financial services. Instead of having a big bank that does everything for everyone, there is now a vast array of fintech companies that are specialising in one critical part of the financial process. The advantage of specialisation during the Industrial Revolution had to do with the improved efficiencies from repeating the same job over time. When it comes to digital processes, the advantage is in much larger sets of data used for very specific purposes. In a fintech network, the presence of a player only focused on financial risk assessment (just one of the many tasks in a bank) can gather information and data flowing from hundreds of different fintech lenders and, over time, can develop more accurate algorithms to benefit the whole ecosystem.

Resulting Trends

These four building blocks are coming together to disrupt the financial services sector and offer novel ways of achieving better results. The combination of big data, AI, improved process automation and networked systems are facilitating various trends that will shape the future of finance. Among those, we believe three warrant particular attention:

- Embedded finance
- Vertical banking
- The rent economy

Embedded Finance

Embedded finance, as we mentioned in the previous chapter, refers to the inclusion of financial services within a non-finance-related experience. Essentially, anyone can add a financial product to what they already do, facilitated by APIs and an ecosystem of fintech players working in partnership. In many ways this is already happening and has been happening for a while. For example, an SME may use Square as a contactless payment system in their store or their website or might be linked up to Stripe to make payments easier for the customer without the business having to create their own backend payment infrastructure. This is common and largely accepted as a useful business tool. It is now so common and widespread that we struggle describing it as an embedded finance solution, but there are now many more options available to businesses to offer far more sophisticated solutions.

> Anyone can add a financial product to what they already do, facilitated by APIs and an ecosystem of fintech players working in partnership.

For example, some fintechs now offer buy-now-pay-later solutions for bricks-and-mortar businesses. A vetinary practice might be aware that some customers may struggle to pay for their pet's care, especially when the treatment runs into surgery or dental work. If that is the case, the customer has the option to scan a QR code at reception, install an app on their phone, input their information and the amount of the total bill and select a payment plan that suits them. The vet is paid the full amount of the transaction (less a small commission) by the fintech company providing this embedded finance solution and the customer repays in the instalments they agreed to.

In this way, finance becomes an ancillary service outside of the core business of the vetinary practice and it becomes an 'originator', finding clients for a fintech that will handle that particular financial service within the customer experience.

There are many different examples of embedded finance integrations. Early examples can be seen in Enterprise Resource Planning (ERP) software and Ecommerce.

ERP Software

ERP software is the software that runs a company effectively. It allows for the integrated management of all the main business processes, often in real time, and can collect, store, manage and interpret data from many business activities (Figure 4.2).

Figure 4.2: Typical ERP System

ERP software systems are clearly tapping into the power of big data, AI and process automation because ERP provides an integrated and continuously updated picture of the business in real time. As the name would suggest, an ERP tracks business resources such as cash, raw materials, production capacity and the status of business commitments such as orders and payroll. All the applications that make up the ERP system share data and managed connections to outside stakeholders. And, increasingly, ERP systems are cloud-based to provide even greater access and efficiencies.

ERP software systems are now also offering in the finance and accounting section access to novel fintech solutions or financial services. Imagine the day of a Finance Director of a large manufacturer. She looks at the ERP dashboard in the morning and a cash flow gap is being flagged by the system because a big order is due to be paid a few days before a large customer is likely to settle their invoice. To manage this shortfall, the Finance Director taps on a fintech company icon in the ERP system that specialises in invoice finance solutions. She then selects an invoice that is already recorded in the system to sell to the fintech company. The ERP system is already connected to the fintech company via an API, so all the data of that invoice is shared. Depending on the agreement and the relationship, the fintech gets access to certain information that is already in the ERP system, which will allow them to decide whether to buy the invoice or not. That data might include Know Your Customer (KYC) information, the payment history of that customer, how long that customer has been buying from the manufacturer, etc. Within twenty-four hours, the transaction is approved, the fintech company buys that single invoice, deposits the total amount less a commission into the manufacturer's bank account thus fixing the shortfall. In the past, the Finance Director would have had to go to the bank, but now there is no need for the bank or the meeting. She doesn't even have to fill in an application form. Instead, the specific financial service required, suggested by an AI algorithm in the ERP, is coming directly to her desk to solve the problem – and it's solved in twenty-four hours.

In this case, the role of the ERP software provider is to offer intelligent suggestions on the most appropriate financial service (AI), source clients for a fintech offering financing (networking) and provide additional data and information on their clients to facilitate risk underwriting (big data).

Ecommerce Platforms

Embedded finance is also accessible via ecommerce marketplaces. We have previously discussed a product called 'buy-now-pay-later' and its function in consumer transactions. However, something similar is taking place in business-to-business (B2B) transactions. Imagine a business marketplace for the purchase of scrap metal. These are often large, cross-border transactions, and you generally do not charge the purchase of ten tonnes of scrap copper on your corporate credit card.

It is in the marketplace's best interest to facilitate the financing of such transactions to maximise the probability of them taking place. This can be done through a B2B 'buy-now-pay-later' solution that allows the buyer to delay the payment for the goods in the future. The fintech company managing the funding service is given access to certain pertinent pieces of information about the buyer and the history on the marketplace and decides whether to approve the credit extension or not. As part of the risk underwriting, the fintech may also be linked to a credit insurance operator and – in real time – can buy insurance protection in case the buyer is not able to pay come ninety days, thus reducing its own credit risk. There are essentially five parties to this exchange: the marketplace, the buyer of metals, the seller, the fintech and the insurance company. If the marketplace was part of an ERP system, there would be six parties all sharing information and providing solutions.

This is one of the new frontiers of fintech, where the checkout for online transactions becomes the entry point for the offering of a financial service called 'buy-now-pay-later'. The service allows consumers or SMEs to partially delay the payment and receive credit from a fintech. The fintech may receive a payment for the service directly from the client or from the ecommerce operator.

Such solutions are already up and running in the market, but in the future we will witness an explosion of use cases where fintechs will allow a greater number of non-financial businesses to transact with their own clients simply by allowing them access to new and novel ways to pay or get financing that makes a transaction more likely. Fintech is already finding new opportunities within the financial ecosystem. Finance will therefore become a business facilitator by helping customers with more flexible finance options at the point of sale, and at the same time it may become a more and more important source of income for those companies acting as an integration party.

Remember, when Amazon was mostly an online bookseller in the early 2000s it launched Amazon Web Services (AWS). Today, AWS makes up the majority of Amazon's profits. In the future, expect more companies, especially in low-margin businesses, to be able to derive an additional chunk of their profit from embedding third-party financial services.

Vertical Banking

Although we don't necessarily think of traditional banking as horizontal banking, it is. Traditional banks, until fairly recently, offered a broad range of products and services to a broad range of customers. The reason they did this was largely economies of scale. Traditional banking has always been a volume business. For many decades, deposits were collected at local branches and loans were disbursed from the same local branches. This necessitated an extensive network of branches to attract the high volumes of customers and business that were necessary to pay for that infrastructure and reach profitability. The branch network was an essential part of the banking business model and it was largely viewed as an asset and a 'moat' that prevented others from competing. Never mind the regulatory hurdles that need to be cleared to be classed as a bank, the network of branches made it impossible for a competitor to replicate because it was prohibitively expensive to create that bank infrastructure.

But as more and more people moved online to do their banking via a website or app, accelerated still further by the Covid pandemic, the branch network became a liability rather than an asset. This is one of the reasons that traditional banks have closed so many branches. They are simply not paying for themselves anymore. Plus, for reasons we outlined in Chapter 1, banks have retreated from the broad market of serving everyone and so they don't need those branches anymore. Their customers are large corporates or high-net-worth individuals in cities, not regional towns. Whilst understandable, this exodus has left far too many people unbanked or underbanked. This is the gap that fintech has stepped into.

Fintech doesn't have a network of branches to pay for. Technology, big data, AI, algorithms and automation are doing what people used to do, so there are lower staff costs.

As a result, fintechs can address the needs of a specific sector because they don't need to focus on volumes to sustain the fixed costs at a branch level. This generates a positive flywheel effect, as addressing the needs of a specific sector allows a fintech to serve that niche much better than a traditional provider of financial services that needs to cater to a much larger set of clients. A fintech company may not need a million clients to be profitable; it can focus in on niche markets and still be profitable with 100,000 clients or even just 10,000. By designing a service specifically to meet the unique needs of that sector, they can offer a far superior experience than a traditional bank constrained by standardised 'one-size-fits-all' products ever could.

> Fintechs can address the needs of a specific sector because they don't need to focus on volumes to sustain the fixed costs at a branch level.

As of 2023, the biggest example of this type of vertical banking is around ecommerce, where there is already a set of products that go from different payment options such as the ability to pay in different currencies, buy-now-pay-later, inventory financing, revenue-based financing and cash advances – all from the same place. Revenue-based financing is essentially a short-term loan that a fintech company is giving to an ecommerce website, usually over five or six months. That loan is repaid as a percentage of the revenues earned by the website. If the website is performing according to plan, the loan is repaid in six months. If sales go down, then the loan automatically takes longer to repay. If sales improve then the loan is paid faster. It's a flexible loan. It is underwritten by the fintech because they have access to a lot of data. For example, they can connect to the website's Shopify account to look at the history of all the transactions in the past and sales growth. They can connect to the advertising accounts via APIs and see if the company's advertising on Google or Facebook is efficient or not, benchmarked to other similar companies. This is big data in action and the increased automation keeps costs lower than the banks. These fintechs are analysing certain types of data that the banks just don't have and have not even thought to look at. No bank for example is looking at advertising efficacy.

Inventory financing is another highly specific ecommerce financial product. A fintech can analyse the inventory of a company and assess how quickly that inventory can be sold on the company website or through marketplaces like Amazon or eBay. This is made possible by a connection from the fintech to the company website and the Amazon Seller Central, for example. Based on that data, the fintech can take a certain level of risk and decide to offer credit against that inventory. The fintech takes delivery of that inventory in a secured warehouse and releases it in batches to the company or marketplace, thus maintaining control over the inventory as collateral. The only difference is that the company has the money for that inventory up front and the goods are sent to the fulfilment centre from a different address. In other words, instead of the company sending the inventory to Amazon for fulfilment it is sent from the fintech instead.

Cash advances can be a game-changer for ecommerce sites too. If you sell on Amazon or any of the large marketplaces, such as Zalando or ASOS, that allow the sale of third-party products, there is almost always a returns policy, which means that the seller does not get the money from sales immediately. Usually, the sellers accumulate credit on these marketplaces and they get paid out every thirty days. There is now a group of fintech companies that are offering a product where they can get connected on your behalf to this marketplace. If there is £30,000 in credit for sales between 1 January and 15 January, the fintech will transfer £25,000 immediately to your account even if the money would not be paid until the end of the month. The seller gets most of their money and can use that to build the business, while the fintech gets paid directly by the marketplace later and earns a commission for taking the risk.

Having access to real-time data represents a major advantage that has not been replicated by traditional financial service providers. With vertical banking, customers and SMEs are going to be able to choose from a far bigger selection of tailor-made solutions that are designed around the needs of their industry and provide convenient ways to do specific tasks in that sector or find solutions designed for that sector. And all these options will be available from one place, with the fintech effectively becoming the specialised bank for that sector. The fintech acts as a hub connecting a vast array of capabilities, easily accessible by clients of that sector when they are needed.

> With vertical banking, customers and SMEs are going to be able to choose from a far bigger selection of tailor-made solutions that are designed around the needs of their industry.

This has already started to happen in ecommerce. Ecommerce is a sector ripe for this advance as there is already relatively easy access to data to assess risk and a rich API network. Over the next twenty years, there will be more and more sectors where fintechs will be able to access the right quantity and quality of data to allow them to offer niche products for specific industries.

Take a restaurant for example: cameras will determine the flow of people in and out of the restaurant. The fintech will get access to data on capacity utilisation and average spend. The restaurant will be able to offer multiple payment options and will have access to 'merchant cash advances', which is the equivalent of revenue-based finance for ecommerce. The fintech could offer inventory financing to keep stocks of long shelf-life items, such as wine. Keeping an extensive wine list is a considerable cost for most restaurants; they need to buy it and then store it in temperature-controlled areas and often some of the really expensive bottles will only sell once every few months. Some fintech companies are already financing such expensive bottles of wine for restaurants in certain locations. If a customer places an order for one of the expensive bottles, the waiter immediately opens an app, orders the bottle and it's couriered over like Deliveroo. Obviously, this doesn't make sense for a $40 bottle of wine but it does for a $1,500 bottle that may only be sold by each restaurant once or twice every few months.

In another, very early-stage, example of vertical banking, fintechs in various jurisdictions are targeting the needs of transport operators by offering revolving cards to manage fuel and other expenses and setting up marketplaces where, in addition to finding business opportunities in the marketplace, operators can sell invoices on activities already performed, at a discount. Combining financial information with GPS data (again, big data in action), these fintechs can provide suggestions to improve profitability while, at the same time, assessing the operating performance of a counterparty more accurately and provide certainty on the execution of past job performance, thus removing part of the fraud risk associated with invoice discounting.

In time, there will be fintech solutions specifically designed for everyone from restaurateurs to plumbers to accountants to designers and beyond, each offering a one-stop shop of financial solutions or capabilities that make their business more efficient. By specialising vertically and leveraging an extensive network of connected parties, these fintechs will be able to operate at low volumes and offer products so tailored to the needs of their clients that traditional banking wouldn't be able to compete with even if they wanted to.

The Rent Economy

Also known as the sharing or collaborative economy, this trend refers to the willingness to borrow or rent an asset rather than owning it. There are several forces driving this trend outside of technological capability. For a start, assets can be very expensive, so ownership is giving way to access. If someone needs a car, does it matter whether they own the car or simply have access to the car when they need it?

The other facilitator, which is linked to cost, is demographic. The Baby Boomers (born 1946–1964) and Gen Xers (born 1965–1980) were all about climbing the corporate ladder, owning stuff and accumulating wealth. Gen Y (born 1981–1995) and younger view the world very differently. They are not as interested in following a scripted path. The old advice of go to school, get good grades, go to university and you'll get a good job is not working out. This approach is certainly no guarantee anymore. Often, they saw how hard their parents worked in companies that demanded loyalty but downsized without a backward glance at the collateral damage it caused. They also saw their parents struggle financially to afford things they never had time to enjoy. These new demographic cohorts are less focused on owning stuff and are more interested in enjoying experiences. They are acutely aware of the many serious problems the world faces, not least the climate crisis, and they want to be part of the solution rather than the problem. The outcome is the sharing economy. Gen Y is the first demographic that has never known a world without the internet.

Gen Z (born 1996–2009) would be astounded at the pains we had to go through to get on the internet back in the 1990s. They are digitally native and are already very used to sharing their lives on social media platforms such as TikTok and Instagram. If it can't be shared, it probably didn't happen!

It's the perfect solution. These demographics can get access to what they want, when they want it (instant gratification) without the financial burden or commitment. And they are not adding to the mountains of waste they already feel bad about (things are refurbished and reused) and they can sleep better knowing they are doing something to solve the environmental mess previous generations have created.

Economic and social theorist Jeremy Rifkin calls this concept the 'collaborative commons', a sharing society where wellbeing is our primary economic goal*. And fintech is certainly stepping into this space.

Instead of buying an asset, fintechs are giving customers the opportunity to rent it or pay a subscription to access it. Then when the customer is finished using it or wants to upgrade,

---

* Rifkin, J., *The Zero Margin Cost Society: The Internet of Things, the Collaborative Commons, and the Eclipse of Capitalism* (Palgrave Macmillan, London, 2015).

they return it to the fintech. That asset gets checked, cleaned or refurbished and it's rented out again. Fintechs are ideally positioned to ride this wave. By acquiring and financing in bulk, they obtain better pricing from suppliers and have a lower cost of funding vs consumers. They can also leverage economies of scale in maintenance and ancillary costs (such as insurance for cars). Thanks to big data, they know what to buy and how to price subscriptions, charging a premium for the convenience and the flexibility.

> **Instead of buying an asset, fintechs are giving customers the opportunity to rent it or pay a subscription to access it.**

We are already seeing this trend with cars, where many fintech companies are offering subscriptions. This is not leasing because when someone leases a car they are locked in and committed to pay for a certain number of years. The fintech subscription model allows a customer to access a car for however long they want. It's flexible. The customer doesn't even necessarily need to decide how long they need the car for upfront. When they are finished with the car, they simple drop it off at an agreed place and hand in the keys. We are seeing the same happening for various products, including consumer electronics. So, instead of having to buy an expensive smartphone, tablet or laptop, consumers can rent it and when they get bored, swap if for a newer model. Rental itself is not new but what changes is the rationale: while in the past rentals gave access to very expensive goods that could not be obtained otherwise, rental today is all about the freedom to change item frequently and the promotion of a circular economy, where used assets are refurbished and rented again at a lower price point. This is a big deal considering that, by some estimates, around 150 million mobile phones are discarded globally each year*. There is little doubt that a good number of those phones could have been refurbished, recycled and used again.

Retailers are also partnering with fintechs to offer these possibilities to customers at the checkout (again an example of embedded finance, this time in the physical world).

Consumers can either buy the monitor or laptop outright (potentially using buy-now-pay-later or point-of-sale financing) or they can rent the product, taking out a subscription.

This business model is also available on more exotic products such as e-bikes, scooters and designer handbags, with new offers being tested daily. There is a company, for example, that allows customers to borrow a certain number of clothing items depending on the level of their subscription. The customer wears the outfit and returns it to the company so they can rent something else. The same is possible for designer handbags, many of which cost thousands of pounds to buy.

The rent economy is a massive trend that is unlikely to recede as more and more fintechs enter the space and give consumers more options to access the goods they want without the cost or commitment.

> The rent economy is a massive trend
> that is unlikely to recede.

---

* Khristopher, Y., 'Total waste generated by throwing mobile phone and devices', AndroidHeadlines (2021).

Digital Lending in the Real World

There is little doubt that fintech is changing the nature of banking, but what will that look like for consumers and SME operators who are currently being left unbanked or underbanked as banks recede from their traditional markets?

Let's go back and compare Libby's experience of managing the day-to-day running of Owen's and how different it will be for James, her son.

As owner of a growing business, Libby has often needed access to more working capital and, like so many SME owners, often that working capital is almost within reach – if only clients would pay their invoices on time. One of the biggest challenges facing SMEs is slow payments. And ironically, the slowest payers are often the largest companies who are in the best position to pay.

As necessity is always the mother of invention, there has been a solution around this for a long time, known as receivables financing or factoring. Receivables financing is a form of secured lending. It can take many forms but, in a nutshell, it refers to the funding of invoices.

Libby worked hard at business development and was never just content to wait for passing traffic to visit her high-street store like her dad was. She set up an ecommerce site and forged mutually beneficial relationships with schools and businesses to supply good-quality shoes as part of a school or business uniform. For example, before the start of each term Libby would sell a bulk order of school shoes to each school at a discount, the school would then offer the discounted shoes to students' parents for slightly more than Libby sold them for, thus raising extra money for the school but also still offering already stretched parents a good deal on school shoes. Libby would invoice each school for the shoes and agree a returns policy with each one on any pairs not sold. But of course, the school didn't always have the money to pay for the shoes upfront and had to recoup some of the cost from students before the payment to Libby could be made. Libby was always generous and gave each school sixty-day terms, meaning they needed to settle within two months. The challenge for Libby was that often she had to buy those shoes herself and so was already out of pocket on the deal. It was a great money-spinner though – if she could just ride out that sixty days and get paid. But often the schools didn't pay at sixty days and some took as much as ninety days, putting a huge financial strain on the business. Libby knew that she would be paid but many a small business has gone under, not because they didn't get paid but because they got paid too late!

Libby also faced another problem. As she ventured into ecommerce, she realised that a larger percentage of her sales was executed on third-party marketplaces. These are much larger ecommerce websites, such as Amazon or Zalando, that attract a lot of consumers and host third-party products such as those sold by Libby. These marketplaces, however, prefer to manage the entire sale process and hence they sell directly to clients and pay the money out to Libby after a certain period of time to cover the risk of clients returning the goods.

Libby investigated working capital solutions to sustain her business, but the process was arduous and time-consuming. Banks have dramatically reduced their physical presence, thus reducing the main advantage her father had when it came to banking: a sound reputation in the territory that gained him enormous respect from the local branch. Now Libby must find information on the most suitable product on the bank website, ask for information via a call centre and file an application online. Solutions are limited to a credit facility with significant fixed costs that make the solution too expensive, largely because Libby's business is seasonal and she does not need the financing for an entire year. Receivables financing seems like a better option. However, once again, the bank wants to serve all the needs of the company and acquire all the receivables, even when this solution is not needed. The lack of flexibility of these standard products puzzles Libby but she is still forced to accept a suboptimal solution. Even worse, since the marketplaces she uses to sell her shoes do not issue an invoice up to the point when payment is due but rather show her a 'credit earned' on her online account, she is not even able to get financing for that!

Libby chose the bank's invoice financing solution and, after a four weeks' journey of paperwork and risk assessment, she would have access to the product. She can now sell invoices to the bank, which then pays her the invoice value less a fee and collects the invoice from each school at sixty days or chase payment after that. Although Libby lost a little on the invoice, the discount reflecting an implied interest rate, it was worth it. She had access to the working capital she needed so she could settle her accounts on the shoes and offer a similar service to another school, thus growing the business.

This type of solution is not new and can be traced back to ancient trade practices, and it is often a potent lifeline for SMEs who may not have the sort of stellar financials that make it easy to access money. The irony of money, and this has been true since the beginning of time, is that it is very easy to access money if your business is already wealthy. It's very unlikely that Coca Cola or Apple have to use receivable financing because their size, wealth and standing mean they can negotiate much better terms. For all the other companies in the world who need access to money or to better manage their cash flow, receivable financing can be a great solution. Instead of looking at the financial health of the business selling the invoices, in this case Libby's, the receivable finance company is often more interested in the financial health and standing of the company paying the invoice, in this case the schools.

If Libby had invoiced Apple or Microsoft for example, those invoices would be very easy to sell because the financial strength of those companies is well known and undisputed. There is no question about whether the receivable financing company will be paid, only when. In Libby's situation, schools are also attractive invoices to purchase because the financial strength (government backing) of the schools makes them very likely to pay. Often the credit merit of the company being invoiced is higher than Libby's, so this approach allows her to tap into that benefit. And it doesn't even matter if Libby goes bankrupt, the invoice is for products that have already been sold and will need to be paid.

One of the familiar patterns of evolution, especially around technological advance, is not only how much cheaper innovations become over time but also how much more accessible and easier to use they become over time. There is always a stumbling block to greater uptake of any solution or technology based on how easy it is to use. We have seen this from computers to the internet to blockchain. Initially, as mentioned in Chapter 3, it's only the innovators or early adopters that can be bothered with new tech or capabilities. Only when it's 'crossed the chasm' and has become either much more functional or accessible does the mass market get involved and it becomes ubiquitous*.

It's all about friction and removing as much friction as possible from the experience of accessing a product, service or capability. The same is true for receivable financing and how it has collided with fintech to create a far better, faster product with far less friction or hassle when trying to use it as a solution.

> **It's all about friction and removing as much friction as possible from the experience of accessing a product, service or capability.**

When James takes over Owen's he always liked his mum's innovation around school and businesses and he respects the relationships she had built up to facilitate this annual boost in revenue. But he is not excited about the process. Luckily for him, those in fintech had already recognised that there were two factors of receivable finance that made it ripe for innovation and improvement as a fintech product.

1. It was operationally intensive. Receivables financing implies spending time to find the right SMEs with good-quality debtors, select the invoices eligible for funding, verify their authenticity by contacting the debtor (this only in case of 'verified' financing), create an account for the repayment of the invoice, handling the cash movements between the various parties (receiving the repayment from the debtor, paying the

---

* Moore, G.A., *Crossing the Chasm: Marketing and selling disruptive products to mainstream customers* (3rd edn, Harper Business, New York, 2014).

debt provider, retaining their own fee and paying back the rest to the SME) and managing delays and defaults. Fintechs have invested a lot in establishing software platforms that have the capability to minimise human intervention and automate as much of the process as possible.

2. Then there is the opportunity to differentiate. Banks always played a major role in providing invoice financing. However, the product has not really evolved over time and instead stayed static. Banks have always known that in this type of financing they hold all the cards; people are desperate. So, the banks generally ask for exclusive relationship and insist on handling 100 per cent of the invoice base. From the bank's perspective, this is to justify the associated operational costs and mitigate the risk of double selling of invoices. But it's not great for the customer. Fintechs came into the market with a much more responsive and flexible solution where companies can access the service with limited commitment and full control over which invoices they want to sell and when, making it a far better solution for business owners.

By the time James is at the helm, receivable finance is a much easier and streamlined process. He opens a financial comparison website that – based on a limited amount of information – displays suggestions on the suitable fintech provider and products he could access to cover his needs. Once the right product is selected, James signs up and provides all the necessary information. This process is highly streamlined. Fintechs know very well that entrepreneurs have limited time availability and in order to close a deal, they need to offer the most efficient onboarding solution. James doesn't even have to input any data or send the financial statements of his business. The app he's using allows him to connect through APIs to his bank account and his accounting system. In this way, the fintech company providing the service can have a clear and up-to-date picture of the financial affairs of the Owens. The decision on approving James's request for an invoice financing facility is made in twenty-four hours and gives him maximum flexibility on how many invoices to sell and how frequently.

Before one of James's children takes over the business from him there will be further improvements and iterations to receivable financing making it even more attractive to SME operators.

Areas of development for the future include:

- **Improved risk underwriting:** Data collection, learning from the past, better assessment of default risk, fraud or dilution. Dilution is when a product or service sold is not as expected and therefore the debtor does not want to pay the full amount of the invoice. AI will allow the fintech to connect more dots and increase accuracy and speed of assessment. And speed will always be one of the key selling points versus traditional banks. Even today, some highly advanced products offer instant credit underwriting. If this is now limited to smaller transactions, in the future we can expect to see it as a standard feature on all financing transactions.
- **Working capital holistic solutions:** We are already seeing the first examples: fintechs develop SaaS products that help SMEs manage their working capital more

effectively. These are easy to use, plug-and-play tools that predict future cash needs based on information on sales and supplies, helping time-constrained entrepreneurs handle invoices and payment delays while optimising purchase orders. In one single console, James will be able to know how much to order and when, who among his clients is more likely to pay late, get access to credit insurance against client defaults, sell invoices to improve cash flow and pay for inventories or suppliers.

- **Blockchain solutions:** One of the main risks of this capability is an invoice being sold twice to two different funders. Of course, the debtor will only pay the invoice once, leaving the other funder out of pocket. In a future where invoices will be issued on a blockchain, each one of them will be a unique item (a NFT that can't be tampered with). Hence, it will only be possible for James to sell an invoice once. An entire ecosystem of companies in a specific sector or supply chain may decide to join forces and have all their invoices issued on a blockchain with mechanisms to incentivise participation and discourage bad behaviour. Entire countries could mandate a full switch to blockchain to issue and record invoices and the benefit could be huge. In Europe the invoice financing market is approximately 2 trillion Euros*.

---

* No Author, 'Annual Factoring Data EU Federation Factoring and Commercial Finance' (2022), https://euf.eu.com/data-statistics/ annual-factoring-data.html#:~:text=The%20total%20turnover%20 for%20the,was%20over%202%20Trillion%20Euros [accessed January 2024].

Even a 1 per cent improvement in interest rates due to this form of risk mitigation could yield a benefit worth 20 billion Euros!

And what about those sales that James executed on marketplaces, where invoices are not issued until they get paid out, but often weeks after the sale took place? Several fintechs are already working on solving this pain point too. Through APIs, a connection is secured to the marketplace, where the entire history of sales of James's products is analysed. The fintech company used by James can see for how long James has been a client of the marketplace, what is the average of his sales, how many times products are returned and the rating James received from his customers. Based on this information, the company offers James an advance on all the money earned but not yet paid out by the marketplace. A special partnership with the marketplace allows the fintech to control the account on which the marketplace itself will make the payment, thus minimising the risk of fraud. Once again, technology has solved a problem that prevented banks from offering a peculiar solution which is experiencing growing demand due to the secular growth in ecommerce.

James is now also able to massively reduce the financial pressure and stress on him and the business when he needs to buy the shoes from the shoe manufacturers so he could offer them to the schools and businesses. He had seen first-hand how stressed his mum got every year, especially prior to new terms, because the business development initiative put a huge amount of pressure on her cash flow. She needed to buy the shoes from the shoe manufacturer to get a big enough discount to make it work, but she had a few tense months during the campaign as the invoices were paid by the schools. And there was always at least one school who paid very late. All of this got even worse when production moved to China where manufacturers required payment on delivery and shipping took an additional four to six weeks.

When he joined the business and was learning the ropes from his mum, James heard about purchase order financing and told her it might be the perfect solution. Purchase order financing is a form of working capital financing that refers to the financing of the purchase price of supply of products or services. Instead of stressing each year like his mother, James used purchase order financing to extend the terms of payments due to shoe manufacturers. After sixty days, when the invoice was due, a fintech would pay the shoe manufacturer the amount and would ask James to repay the full amount advanced with a delay of ninety days, giving him a little more breathing space. This is technically a ninety-day loan and allows James to pay for the bulk shoe order in 150 days (60 + 90 days). During this period, James can now conduct his annual school shoe push to local schools, sell the shoes and, with the proceeds, repay the fintech company offering this product. In essence, this is an unsecured short-term loan. Risk of fraud is mitigated by the fact that money is not given directly to James but it is paid into the account of the shoe manufacturer. Funds can't be used for any other purpose except the purchase of the shoes offered.

Again, fintechs have been able to gain a foothold in this space because of the product innovation, flexibility and speed. Banks do offer general working capital facilities but they take a long time to provide funding. Traditional working capital facilities come with costs that make the transaction profitable for banks but not necessarily convenient for customers, especially if the facility is only used once or twice a year. Unsurprisingly, it was not always convenient for smaller companies like Libby's to access this facility through the bank. But fintechs changed that. They offer products where risk underwriting is notably performed in a matter of a day, giving clients like James flexible access to funding with limited fixed costs. Plus, the process is fully automated and much more streamlined than seeking something similar with a bank.

In the future, James will benefit from far more niche and specialised offers, including a host of different buy-now-pay-later options. In the years to come, an ever-increasing amount of B2B transaction will take place online. Hence, B2B buy-now-pay-later will experience a significant development. And this capability will be available to all the players in James's supply chain: on the one hand, parents of the children who are buying the shoes will be able to split the payment through a consumer buy-now-pay-later capability they can access on their phone; on the other, the B2B versions will allow SMEs to delay the payment of their invoices, all done through a seamless online experience at a checkout in the wholesale ecommerce website set up by the Chinese manufacturer.

By the time James's children join the business, assuming they want to, a vast network of automated fintech solutions connected on the platform economy will be available to the business to meet just about any and every finance-related problem.

Chapter 5:
The Evolution of Digital Assets

In the digital lending space, the first steps were taken to move paper-based systems onto computers and eventually online. This move facilitated the collection of more data and more accurate information and created a whole host of storage, cost and time efficiencies. The evolution of digital assets has, up to a point, been similar. Digital assets such as photos, manuscripts, documents or data have been around as long as there have been computers to store them. Those types of digital assets have made the same journey, from paper-based physical assets onto computers and eventually online. However certain technological innovations created a Big Bang Event that changed what was possible in the digital asset space in radical ways.

These new digital asset capabilities promoted a completely new way of doing things that were not just systematic improvements to the way things had been done in the past, they marked something else entirely. If you think about this like the advent of the railway, the ability to lay rail tracks across a country to create a transport network revolutionised physical transport and global trade. Since the initial innovation of rail tracks, all sorts of improvements to the tracks, the network, the trains using those tracks and the reason for using those tracks has delivered significant, albeit incremental, improvements to the cost and efficiency of rail transportation. In the digital assets space, we are now at the point where we have a reasonably good technology for 'laying rail tracks' and we are now focusing on all those incremental improvements that, over time, will open new use cases and will lead to the creation of new industries.

> These new digital asset capabilities promoted
> a completely new way of doing things.

The most relevant technology innovations that are transforming digital assets include:

- Blockchain
- Digital ledger technology
- Smart contracts and Decentralised Applications (DApps)

Blockchain

As mentioned in Chapter 3, the first ever blockchain, block-chain 1.0, was Bitcoin. On 31 October 2008, right in the middle of the most serious financial crisis since World War II, a nine-page white paper entitled, *Bitcoin: A Peer-to-Peer Electronic Cash System*, was published under the pseudonym Satoshi Nakamoto. An abstract of the paper, published to a cryptography mailing list, read:

A purely peer-to-peer version of electronic cash would allow online payments to be sent directly from one party to another without going through a financial institution. Digital signatures provide part of the solution, but the main benefits *are lost if a trusted third party is still required to prevent double-spending. We propose a solution to the double-spending problem using a peer-to-peer network. The network timestamps transactions by hashing them into an ongoing chain of hash-based proof-of-work, forming a record that cannot be changed without redoing the proof-of-work*[*].

On 3 January 2009, the Bitcoin network was launched with Nakamoto mining the first block on the Bitcoin block-chain, known as the genesis block. You might remember from Chapter 1 that embedded into the genesis block was a headline from *The Times* on the same day: *The Times Jan/03/2009 Chancellor on brink of second bailout for banks*. As well as timestamping the genesis block of Bitcoin, the reference is thought to be a reminder of the urgent need for this *new purely peer-to-peer version of electronic cash* that Nakamoto had suggested a year earlier.

Other users were invited to mine Bitcoin, and they did. Not only was this the first cryptocurrency (more on those shortly) but it represented a seismic shift in the financial world, although not many people realised it at the time.

> Not only was Bitcoin the first cryptocurrency but it represented a seismic shift in the financial world.

To mine Bitcoin, anyone could simply download software to their computer to solve increasingly complex maths problems and receive a certain number of Bitcoins in exchange for the computational effort associated with validating transactions

---

[*]   Cooke, G.C., *Web3: The End of Business as Usual* (Whitefox, London, 2023).

(exchanges of Bitcoins from one user to another). Those transactions were recorded on the Bitcoin blockchain.

Unlike the Central Banks, who simply print money through quantitative easing when they need to, scarcity was built into Bitcoin by design. There will only ever be 21 million Bitcoin that will be created by miners. Each mining computer represents a node in the Bitcoin network and a representation of the entire Bitcoin blockchain is contained in each of those nodes. Miners validate each single transaction, which is recorded on the Bitcoin blockchain and verified by all the other nodes in the network. This is all done by algorithms and computational power rather than human beings. Once consensus is found on a set of transactions, they are all grouped in a 'block'. This new block is uploaded automatically to all the nodes and becomes an integral part of the blockchain. This process of validation of all transactions through a block system, makes it next to impossible to hack or change because the rest of the network would recognise an unverified change. The immutability of the blockchain and the inability to tamper with the information represents one of the most useful characteristics of this new technology.

Bitcoin was the first example of a blockchain but there are now many more.

Although the creation of the blockchain represents a huge advance and the laying of new, very different, tracks in the digital world, it is interesting to note that it is still an example of the Innovator's Dilemma.

'The Innovator's Dilemma' is a concept from a book by the late Harvard Business School professor Clayton Christensen, which explores the challenges that successful companies face when dealing with disruptive innovation. Christensen argued that well-established companies can fail, not because they don't innovate, but because they fail to adapt to disruptive innovations that might initially seem irrelevant to them or be less profitable or significant.

The main premise of the Innovator's Dilemma can be summarised as follows:

- **Sustaining Innovation:** Successful companies focus on sustaining innovation, which involves incremental improvements to existing products and services to meet the demands of their existing customers. These innovations are usually well-received by the market and contribute to the company's continued success. This is how most improvements are made – they are linear and they are bought into and embraced over time as a logical progression.

- **Disruptive Innovation:** Disruptive innovations, on the other hand, usually target niche markets. These innovations may not appeal to the company's existing customer base, or to investors, as they may seem inferior or irrelevant compared to the established products. However, over time, disruptive innovations can improve and eventually surpass the performance of existing products, capturing larger market shares.

- **The Dilemma:** The dilemma faced by established companies (and investors) is that, while they excel at sustaining innovation and meeting the demands of their current customers, they often struggle to embrace disruptive innovations that may disrupt their own business models. The reluctance to invest in and prioritise disruptive technologies can lead to the decline of these companies in the long run, as new, more agile competitors embrace and dominate the emerging markets. We can see this play out on a massive scale in the financial services sector. The incumbent banks have been slow to appreciate the disruptive nature of blockchain and how the emergence of this technology (and others) poses a very real existential threat to their existence or at the very least a significant risk to their expected profit margins.

We can also see the stages play out for disruptive innovations across the centuries. Although there were some people who loved the idea of cars, most didn't. Most would-be or at least potential customers disliked the noise and dust clouds and considered them a physical threat to pedestrians, cyclists and horses. In Vermont in the US, they passed a law requiring a person to walk in front of the car waving a red flag! In Illinois someone stretched a length of steel cable across the road to stop 'the devil wagons'. Some cities banned cars outright*. However, disruptive innovators like Henry Ford had the courage to propose something that might not appeal to their customer base on Day One. 'If I had asked people what they wanted, they would have said faster horses.' This sentence encapsulates the Innovator's Dilemma perfectly, but Ford pressed on and changed the world of transportation forever. Cars didn't make sense – until they did.

Fast forward to mainframe computers and one of the biggest challenges was storage capacity. Moore's Law was holding firm: the number of transistors in an integrated circuit was doubling every two years. As technology progressed,

---

* No Author, '100 Years ago, some people were really hostile to the introduction of the automobile', Dangerous Minds (2013).

storage capacity increased exponentially for several decades. Customers liked the larger storage capacity but there was a divergent approach that was producing smaller, more portable storage options. Most people were confused by this innovation – it didn't make sense commercially. Until it did.

Fast forward again to the internet and most people who looked at it couldn't work out what all the fuss was about because there were countless off-line solutions that were far superior to what was being offered online at the time. Why create a website that looked like a high school project when you would create beautifully designed brochure offline? Or why struggle with poor word processing options or spreadsheets online when Microsoft already had a great suite of products that did those jobs well. Again, the internet didn't make sense – until it did.

In each of these cases and countless others, the critical benefit or opportunity of the disruptive innovation is not initially appreciated by would-be customers, businesses or investors, so they dismiss it. As German philosopher Arthur Schopenhauer once said, *All truth passes through three stages. First, it is ridiculed. Second, it is violently opposed. Third, it is accepted as being self-evident.* The same happens with disruptive innovations.

Whether cars, smaller storage drives or the internet, the emergence of the innovation is often ridiculed and opposed, although not necessarily violently. Most of the time it's just ridiculed and ignored. It doesn't make sense to people. Why would someone want a car when they already have a horse-drawn carriage? Why would someone want smaller storage capacity when everyone else is clamouring for more storage? Why would someone want to use the internet when you could do the same thing off-line so much better? They dismiss it because they are almost always comparing it to what already exists rather than to what this new technology would lead to.

And, to be fair, it is easy to make the mistake because in each case the new disruptive innovation is worse in almost every way in comparison to what already exists, except for one specific dimension or characteristic*.

But, over time, it is that one specific dimension or characteristic that becomes its greatest advantage – convenience for cars, portability for small hard drives and networked access for the internet become the one thing that people start to value and new markets are attracted to the disruptive innovation *because* of that single dimension. Sometime after, the disruptive innovation becomes self-evident.

We are not quite at the self-evident stage with blockchain but it's fast approaching. For blockchain, there are countless things that can be done more efficiently, faster and cheaper off-chain. But blockchain technology comes with some unique characteristics.

- **Trust:** The process of validating transactions is assigned to a large network of interconnected computers. The system does not rely on a single trusted institution for validation, like for a credit card network.
- **Resilience:** The system is decentralised and does not rely on a single actor to function. Each node in the network could be easily removed without prejudice to the functioning of the system. This reduces reliance on a single entity like a Central Bank or tech company, potentially lowering the risk of censorship or central points of failure.

---

* Harrison, C., 'The HCI Innovator's Dilemma', IX Interactions (2018).

- **Security:** Once added to a block, transactions are permanently recorded on the blockchain and they become nearly impossible to alter. Hacking is made virtually impossible by the distributed nature of the underlying database. This immutability provides a high level of security and trust, as it prevents tampering with historical records.
- **Speed and Cost:** By eliminating intermediaries, transactions on a blockchain settle almost instantaneously at a fraction of the cost. If, as an example, we compare the cost of traditional remittances to a personal wallet-to-wallet transaction, the advantages are staggering. A report commissioned by fintech company, Wise, in 2022 showed that the cost of remittances during 2021 was averaging 6.2 per cent of the value of the transfer. The United Nations Sustainable Development Goals includes the aspiration of remittance costs of 3 per cent or lower, but these costs have only decreased by 1 per cent since 2015. Fintech is changing that by allowing consumers to keep more of their money. If, for example, the UN aspiration had been achieved in 2022 it would have saved consumers in the G20 $5 billion in fees[*].
- **Visibility and Transparency:** While personal identities are never shared in blockchain transactions, each transaction is publicly visible. As an example, on the Bitcoin blockchain, information about the wallet sending money, the wallet receiving it and the amount involved can be retrieved at any time.

---

[*] VanBulck, M., 2022 *Remittances Report: Can G20 countries that are net senders of remittances achieve the UN goal of reducing costs to 3% by 2030?*, https://wise.com/community/remittancereport2022 [accessed January 2024].

- **Resilience to Outages:** Since blockchain is a distributed network, it is more resilient to outages and technical failures compared to centralised systems. This feature is critical for maintaining uninterrupted access to essential data and services.

Like all disruptive innovation, there is always a trade-off, especially at the start. But the advantages of the decentralised system are enormous, and it is this capability that has created an enormous flourishing of innovation in the fintech space, especially as the costs to access the blockchain continue to drop.

As co-founder of DeepMind and Inflection AI, Mustafa Suleyman, rightly points out, *Almost every foundational technology ever invented from pickaxes to ploughs, pottery to photography, phones to planes, and everything in between, follows a single, seemingly immutable law: it gets cheaper and easier to use, and ultimately it proliferates, far and wide*[*].

The genie is out the bottle in terms of the blockchain and it is never going back in. Companies, consumers and investors can either embrace the change and make it work for them or dismiss it and be left behind. It may have been possible to dismiss the Bitcoin blockchain as a niche product in a niche sector, but it didn't take long for other people to see the potential of the blockchain and digital ledger technologies more broadly.

> The genie is out the bottle in terms of the blockchain and it is never going back in.

---

[*] Sulleyman, M. and Bhasker, M., *The Coming Wave* (Vintage, London, 2023).

Digital Ledger Technologies

Although the term *digital ledger technologies* (DLT) is often used interchangeably with blockchain, they are not the same.

Every blockchain is a DLT but not all DLTs are blockchains. DLT is a broader term that refers to any system that records, shares and stores data across a network available to multiple participants. DLTs eliminate the need to rely on traditional centralised databases. Like the blockchain, the decentralised aspect of DLTs make it more secure. When a company or organisation relies on a centralised database, that database can be hacked, and we see this with major corporations all the time.

Between 2013 and 2016, a team of Russian hackers stole personally identifiable information on over 3 billion Yahoo! user accounts. In January 2021, 60,000 global companies were affected by an attack on Microsoft Exchange email servers, one of the biggest servers in the world. The hackers were able to exploit four different 'zero-day vulnerabilities' to gain unauthorised access to the email of small businesses and local governments. A zero-day vulnerability is an unpatched security weakness that is unknown to the software, hardware or firmware developer. In July of the same year, the US government, along with the FBI, accused China of the data breach and Microsoft named Hafnium, a Chinese state-sponsored hacker group as the group behind the attack[*].

---

[*] Chin, K., 'Biggest Data Breaches in US History', UpGuard (Updated 2023).

These incidents are not alone and many more organisations have fallen prey to hackers, including Facebook, LinkedIn, J.P. Morgan Chase, Home Depot, Adobe, eBay, Capital One Bank, Tesco, British Airways, Equifax and Lloyd's Bank. These are all very large companies with very smart people, deep pockets and sophisticated resources dedicated to preventing these breaches and yet hacks still happen because a centralised system will always have a single point of breach. With DLT this is not possible unless cybercriminals manage to breach all the computers inside the network at the same time, a task that would be impossibly expensive to pull off.

Because the first blockchain to gain global adoption was Bitcoin and Bitcoin runs on a decentralised network, it is often assumed that all blockchains are decentralised, but they're not. Blockchains have evolved and they record data across multiple computers in a network, but that network can be made up of a very large or a small number of nodes. In a centralised blockchain network, a single entity or group of people or organisations control who can join the network and they will determine what rights members have in the centralised network. This is very different from a decentralised network, where anyone can view and validate ledger processes. For example, because Bitcoin is opensource, anyone can download the Bitcoin blockchain, become a 'node' and run the Bitcoin 'full node wallet' software that verifies all the rules of Bitcoin. DLTs like directed acyclic graph (DAG), hashgraph and holochain, are also almost always decentralised.

The immutable, decentralised and transparent nature of blockchains make them incredibly useful for recording important events, especially in a post-truth world, managing important records that should not be tampered with, processing transactions, tracking asset ownership or voting. There is a gravity attached to each of these uses that makes accuracy and the need to avoid fraud and corruption extremely important, but not all information or events fall into that category.

In some cases, it's just important to have a safe digital record of the information but that can be achieved simply through distributed databases, without the on-chain capability. There was talk, for example, of having social media information stored in a blockchain, but most of us would agree that most of the information on social media doesn't really warrant the security of a blockchain. Especially when one of the major issues of blockchains, especially those using 'proof-of-work' (PoW) verification techniques, is the high energy usage. PoW was the original way that blocks on the blockchain were verified. Powerful computers would be asked to solve very difficult, unique mathematical equations based on an advanced form of mathematics called *cryptography* to verify if the transaction was authentic. The fundamental idea behind PoW is that the network reaches consensus through the proof of expended computational effort. The first miner to solve the puzzle gets the privilege of adding a new block of transactions to the blockchain and is rewarded with newly created cryptocurrency coins and transaction fees. This process ensures that participants in the network must demonstrate they've put in genuine computational work, making it prohibitively expensive for malicious actors to control the network.

PoW is very secure but uses a lot of electricity. According to the Cambridge Electricity Consumption Index, Bitcoin uses 155.86 TWh per year. That's more than double all the lighting and TV costs of the US for a year (120 TWh) and a little less than global copper mining (167 TWh)*.

As such, one of the most damning criticisms levelled at Bitcoin and crypto more widely is that it is not environmentally friendly. Although it is a valid criticism there is nuance: not all energy use is equal, something recognised by Coinshare's Chief Strategy Officer, Meltem Demirors, who suggested that Bitcoin and other energy-intensive cryptocurrencies could be viewed as batteries because it 'makes energy mutable, portable, storable and transferable by turning it into money[†]'. Clearly, if a large Bitcoin mining operation is drawing power from the grid, it is costly and potentially puts a strain on the grid that impacts other users. But if the mining operation is using wind or solar power in an otherwise inhospitable landscape then it could be very cost-effective. The irony of solar and wind energy is that often these alternative energy producers are in challenging places such as remote mountainous regions or deserts. Whilst the energy produced may be green and renewable, that energy still needs to be transported across often thousands of miles of new pylons made with concrete and steel. Creating a Bitcoin mining operation using solar energy in the outback of Australia would therefore be far more environmentally friendly than creating that pylon infrastructure, not to mention the fact that the process of getting energy onto the grid using existing infrastructure loses about a third of the energy from the original source[‡]. Bitcoin mining in such areas

---

* https://ccaf.io/cbnsi/cbeci/comparisons
† Belizaire, J., 'Bitcoin Is a Better Battery', Medium (2021).
‡ Wirfs-Brock, J., 'Lost in Transmission: How Much Electricity Disappears Between A Power Plant And Your Plug?', insideenergy.org (2015).

therefore creates an opportunity to transform an abundant natural resource, wind or the sun, into cryptocurrency that could then be spent to improve the local area or by local governments. Additionally in this vein, some blockchain projects focus on environmental sustainability, enabling more efficient energy distribution and even incentivising renewable energy production through various mechanisms.

Although the Bitcoin battery is a novel and valid idea, the fact remains that anything using PoW is still using a lot of energy that is coming from various national grids. Clearly this is an issue that needs to be solved, and so PoW is being replaced by 'proof-of-stake' (PoS) in many blockchains. Instead of mining, PoS validation increasingly comes from users buying in (owning a stake) to approve transactions. They are effectively saying, I am willing to stake my own money as proof that this information or transaction is accurate and valid. There is no point in doing that if the transaction is not accurate because the rest of the nodes in the network will prove it is not valid and the stake will be lost, whereas, once the transaction is verified, the stake is returned along with a little extra as confirmation and validation[*]. And the more coins a participant stakes, the higher their chances of being chosen as a validator.

PoS replaces the resource-intensive, puzzle-solving process of PoW with a deterministic selection process, reducing energy consumption and enabling faster transaction processing. Validators have a financial incentive to act honestly because they can lose their staked assets if they validate fraudulent transactions. This concept of 'skin in the game' aligns the

---

[*] Cooke, G.C., *Web3: The End of Business as Usual* (Whitefox, London, 2023).

interests of validators with the network's security. PoW is known for its robustness and security but is criticised for its environmental impact. PoS aims to provide a more energy-efficient and scalable alternative while still incentivising network security through economic means.

Blockchains that have already moved to PoS, such as Ethereum 2.0, have reported a drop in energy use of 99.95 per cent[*]. And it is the emergence of Ethereum 2.0 that facilitated the next building block – smart contracts (more on these in a moment).

Another example is Cardano, a blockchain platform designed for smart contracts and decentralised applications. Validators are incentivised to act honestly because they have a financial stake in the form of ADA tokens at risk. By using PoS, Cardano achieves energy savings while still ensuring network security and decentralisation.

DLTs don't always use PoW or even PoS consensus mechanisms. Hashgraph, for example, uses the Gossip protocol to achieve consensus in distributed systems. This mechanism is quick, fast and secure in validating transactions. Other types of DLTs, like holochain, use the distributed hash table (DHT) consensus mechanism to maintain data integrity[†]. Without going too much into technical detail, these are all different technological solutions to allow the recording and distribution of information on a network. Each has advantages and disadvantages, but what is important is the fact that the mere existence of these technologies will, over time,

---

[*] Dillet, R., 'Ethereum switches to proof-of-stake consensus after completing', The Merge Techcrunch (2022).

[†] Shafii, K., 'Blockchain vs. DLT (Distributed Ledger Technology) Explained', Consensus (2023).

allow business uses to be developed taking advantage of their intrinsic characteristics.

DLTs don't always use PoW or even PoS consensus mechanisms.

Smart Contracts and DApps

Following the launch of Bitcoin, there was a flurry of cryptocurrency or 'altcoin' activity, most notably, the launch of Litecoin in 2011, touted as 'silver to Bitcoin's gold', Peercoin and Ripple in 2012 and Dogecoin in 2013. Each had their own unique features, use cases and underlying technologies but they were all purely currency applications. However, Ethereum, launched in 2015, was different.

A year before, in 2014, Gavin Wood, co-founder of Ethereum, wrote a blog post where he sketched out his view of the new digital landscape in Web 3.0. He suggested that Web 3.0, would herald a *reimagination of the sorts of things we already use the web for, but with a fundamentally different model for the interactions between parties.* Wood went on to suggest that, *Information that we assume to be public, we publish. Information that we assume to be agreed, we place on a consensus-ledger. Information that we assume to be private, we keep secret and never reveal.* In this vision, all communication is encrypted and identities are hidden. *In short, we engineer the system to mathematically enforce our prior assumptions, since no government or organization can reasonably be trusted*[*].

---

[*] Stackpole, T., 'What is Web3?', *Harvard Business Review* (2022).

Again, remember this is at a time when the fallout of the GFC is still very much being felt. Banks are no longer trusted third parties but simply for-profit financial intermediaries. And governments have not fared much better. People were angry about the government bailouts, which often led to stifling austerity where everyday people were made to suffer for the hubris and greed of large financial institutions. In addition, no one was held accountable. In the US, 324 mortgage lenders, loan officers and real estate brokers were convicted but not a single Wall Street CEO was prosecuted for their role in the GFC. In the UK the CEO of Barclays and three other executives were charged with conspiracy to commit fraud and provision of unlawful financial assistance but they were all cleared of charges*. Iceland was the only exception, with the Icelandic government prosecuting the CEOs of three of their larger banks and twenty-three other banks†.

As far as the public was concerned, there was clearly evidence that neither banks nor governments could be trusted!

Ethereum was a significant development in the crypto-currency space. Although it built on Bitcoin's innovation, Ethereum offered some significant differences. While both Bitcoin and Ethereum offer the use of digital money (Bitcoin and ETH respectively) without payment providers, third-party intermediaries or banks, Ethereum offers far more flexibility. The only thing the Bitcoin blockchain can record

---

* Verity, A., 'Former Barclays executives cleared of fraud charges', BBC (2020).
† Scannell, K. and Milne, R., 'Who was convicted because of the global financial crisis?', *Financial Times* (2017).

is Bitcoin transactions but with the Ethereum blockchain the sky's the limit. Ethereum was the world's first programmable blockchain. It is a decentralised, open-source blockchain platform that enables the creation and deployment of smart contracts and Decentralised Applications (DApps).

Although the term *smart contract* was first introduced by computer scientist and cryptographer Nick Szabo in the 1990s, his conceptualised vision of self-executing contracts with the terms directly written into code was just theoretical until Ethereum co-founders Vitalik Buterin and Gavin Woods made it a reality. They recognised that the Bitcoin blockchains scripting language allowed for basic programmable conditions that laid the groundwork for more sophisticated smart contracts platforms. Ethereum was that platform and represented a significant leap in the evolution of smart contracts through the introduction of a more versatile and expressive scripting language called Solidity.

A smart contract is exactly as Szabo envisaged: a self-executing contract with the terms of the agreement directly written into code on the blockchain. These contracts automatically execute and enforce the terms when predefined conditions are met. Smart contracts enable a wide range of applications, from decentralised finance (De-Fi) to token issuance and more.

> Smart contracts enable a wide range of applications, from decentralised finance (De-Fi) to token issuance and more.

In the off-chain, off-line world if we wanted to sell you an asset, let's say a valuable painting, both parties would need to hire a lawyer. The lawyers would talk – probably quite slowly, as they charge by the hour – and, eventually, we would agree a price for the painting. The buyer would deposit the money in the lawyer's account and the painting would then be verified and authenticated. Once it was authenticated, contracts would be signed and the money would be released to us less any fees to the lawyer, appraiser or any other relevant third party. Smart contracts effectively do away with those intermediaries and the contract can be fully executed digitally.

Say, instead of wanting to sell you a painting we decided to sell you a non-fungible token (NFT) representing some digital art. A piece of code (a so-called 'smart contract') would be created, using *if . . . then . . .* statements to authorise and release the funds, as ETH in exchange for the NFT while recording the transaction on the blockchain. In other words, the smart contract might say, in code, if the agreed amount is transferred into wallet X by a certain time then the NFT is to be released to wallet Y. If the first action does not take place, the contract expires and the NFT is not released to the new wallet. And, because Ethereum has since developed the Ethereum Virtual Machine (EVM), there is a runtime environment that enables the execution of smart contracts. It is a Turing-complete virtual machine, meaning it can execute any script or program if there are enough computational resources. This is clearly a very simple example of a transaction, but applications may be more complex and peculiar to blockchain, such as flash loans.

A flash loan is a particular type of loan where money is borrowed and repaid within the same transaction block, typically in as little as fifteen seconds. What would be the purpose of borrowing money for just fifteen seconds? One reason is cryptocurrency arbitrage across different exchanges. Let's assume that a cryptocurrency is priced higher against Bitcoin on an exchange with respect to another. An arbitrageur may create a smart contract that would allow to borrow a certain number of Bitcoins, sell them in exchange for the cryptocurrency and then sell such cryptocurrency on the exchange where the price is higher, thus pocketing a small Bitcoin profit. The smart contract is designed in such a way that the overall transaction takes place only if all the underlying transactions take place, or else nothing happens.

What we have just described is an example of a full on-chain smart contract. But what about a situation where the *if . . . then . . .* logic of a smart contract depends on an event that takes place off-chain? Clearly there is still a divide between the on-chain and off-chain world. But huge strides are being made in connecting them. Oracles are part of that solution. An oracle is a source of information that provides real-world data to a smart contract on a blockchain or DLT acting as a bridge: fetching and delivering external data to smart contracts.

For example, if a smart contract needs to make decisions based on the outcome of a real-world event (such as weather conditions, stock prices or sports results), it may rely on an oracle to provide that information. The oracle retrieves the external data and feeds it into the smart contract, allowing the contract to execute predetermined actions based on the received information.

Smart contracts can also interact with oracles to determine the impact of external factors on the value of financial assets. For example, financing for goods being shipped from China to Europe could interact with an off-chain oracle, tapping into GPS tracking information to determine where the goods were and recalibrate the risk profile along the route. Another example in agricultural financing might be assessing the risk on production as a function of weather patterns, tracked in real time to determine a change in the price of a financial asset – all happening automatically without an intermediary.

Oracles are playing an increasingly crucial role in enabling smart contracts to interact with real-world data, events or systems that exist outside the DLT. This is important because blockchains and DLTs are often isolated from external information for security and trust reasons. Oracles bridge this gap by fetching and delivering external data to smart contracts, allowing them to make decisions or trigger actions based on real-world events. There is clearly a trade-off to make here: the system is not completely robust anymore because of the reliance on the external oracle, but the benefit is tangible in the ability to connect on-chain and off-chain events. Over time, a lot more effort will be put on assuring the reliability of oracles to make sure that their centralised nature does not defy the purpose of a decentralised transaction. We are still at the beginning of that journey.

The flexibility and programmability of the Ethereum blockchain (and others like it) are creating an ecosystem where developers can build decentralised applications (DApps) and financial products such as flash loans, utilising smart contracts to execute code on the Ethereum blockchain. Unlike traditional apps, DApps run on a peer-to-peer network of computers (nodes) rather than on centralised servers. This decentralised nature brings several of the advantages previously mentioned. As a technology, DApps have been a game-changer in fintech but we are still just scratching the surface of possible applications.

From a technology standpoint, as posited by the Innovator's Dilemma, blockchain, DLTs, smart contracts and DApps may appear to take a technological step back in that they offer capabilities that are already delivered off-chain. But they achieve these outcomes in a very different way, with certain advantages that are often not yet fully understood by business owners or investors. To understand this concept, we may refer to the early experimentations at the beginning of the World Wide Web era. A very early website may have been a static page describing a business. Today, that very same business can sell its products online, provide customer service, receive CVs and a myriad of other things through its website. The underlying technology has not changed, but over the decades we have developed many more applications and use cases for that underlying technology.

As is often the case with new technologies, we face new trade-offs. The level of security achievable through blockchain requires the interaction of numerous nodes on an extensive network, which creates redundancies in the process. Every time something is redundant, it comes with increased inefficiency; that is, it is not the fastest and cheapest way to perform a computation. However, the benefits gained from the resultant DApps, via smart contracts on the blockchain or other DLTs, more than counterbalance these inefficiencies. Such benefits open numerous new applications and capabilities in the world of finance that are not possible without these technological innovations. But, remember, this is the Innovator's Dilemma in action, so it is still relatively easy to ignore or dismiss these new opportunities as a fad or flash in the pan, thus missing out on the long-term impact they will likely have.

Resulting Trends

It is the combination of these innovations or technological building blocks that are creating huge opportunities in the fintech space and beyond, and they point to several very interesting trends for cryptocurrencies, tokenisation and De-Fi.

Cryptocurrency

One of the big fears following the bank bailouts and increased quantitative easing (QE) by Central Banks after the GFC was that the massive injection of capital would lead to out-of-control inflation. This, coupled with general economic uncertainty, led several well-known investors and financial figures to increase their exposure to gold. For example, George Soros, currency speculator and philanthropist, has historically shown interest in gold as a hedge against inflation. John Paulson, who successfully bet against subprime mortgages during the GFC, invested heavily in gold-related assets after the 2009 market recovery, including gold mining companies and exchange-traded funds (ETFs) through his hedge fund, Paulson & Co. David Einhorn, founder of Greenlight Capital also expressed his views on gold as a hedge against what he perceived as reckless monetary policies. He has often advocated for owning gold as a form of 'currency protection'. And, finally, Jim Rogers, well-known investor and co-founder of the Quantum Fund with George Soros expressed concerns about fiat currencies (more on those in a moment) and inflation, leading him to favour tangible assets like gold. In short, very smart people who knew what they were talking about were extremely concerned about the inflationary impact of QE.

The world was still very much reeling from the fallout of the GFC and a huge amount of trust was lost in the banks, large financial institutions and governments, as explored earlier. And this loss of trust is especially pertinent when you consider how money has evolved over the span of thousands of years, reflecting the needs and complexities of human societies.

Initially trade was made possible by the barter system, where people would exchange goods and services directly without a common medium of exchange. However, it wasn't very efficient or convenient. Over time, commodity money emerged as the solution where the 'money' had intrinsic value often derived from the precious metals like gold or silver that were contained in the coins. These commodities were widely accepted as a medium of exchange. But as trade and commerce expanded, something else was needed as precious metals are precious largely because they are relatively rare, which they certainly were before industrial mining. These metal coins didn't really have much intrinsic value but they represented a standardised form of commodity money and were more convenient for trade. Governments and rulers started minting coins, establishing a system of authority over their currency.

As trade continued to grow, carrying large quantities of metal coins became impractical. It was also increasingly dangerous. Paper money emerged as a more portable, convenient and safer form of currency. The paper money was, however, backed by a commodity like gold or silver held in reserve. This 'representative money' provided a more flexible way to facilitate transactions and was considered safe – or certainly safer – than metal coins.

Over time, many countries moved away from the gold or silver standard, and fiat money emerged. A fiat currency is simply the currency issued by a government. Incidentally the term 'fiat' comes from the Latin word meaning 'let it be done' or 'it shall be'. This is important, as it harks back to the emergence of fiat money being essentially based on trust. Fiat money is not backed by a physical commodity but relies on the trust and confidence of the people and the issuing government. People essentially chose to trust that the piece of paper that they had in their hand was worth the denomination on the note.

The GFC did a huge amount of damage to the global economy but it also decimated that trust both in Central Banks who issue fiat currency and the governments who authorise it.

Bitcoin, the first cryptocurrency, stepped into the void left by these events. Bitcoin was impervious to inflation because scarcity was programmable through software, leaving price growth to become a function of adoption. While supply follows specific rules, demand is always a function of adoption.

> Bitcoin was impervious to inflation because
> scarcity was programmable through software.

The programmable scarcity came from the fact that there was only ever going to be 21 million Bitcoin produced. Each Bitcoin is divisible by 100 million so that's 21 million multiplied by 100 million Satoshis (a Satoshi is to Bitcoin what pence is to the pound or cents are to the Euro). But it's still a fixed amount of Bitcoin. Bitcoin was also coming into the system at a very specific pace based on a predefined formula, so there was no massive influx of Bitcoin into the system for any reason, unlike fiat currency via QE. It wasn't owned by anyone or by any government. Bitcoin was mined and recorded on the network and, once the transaction was verified, all the nodes in the network were updated, making it very hard to hack. It wasn't possible to undo a transaction or reverse a transaction; everything was recorded on the Bitcoin blockchain permanently. You can imagine how, on the back of the GFC, such characteristics were seen as a credible alternative to fiat currency.

Despite the presence of a fertile ground, when Bitcoin started it didn't get much attention from anyone other than those who believed that the world was heading into a massive currency debasement because of the Central Banks and those who were intellectually invested in Nakamoto's idea of a peer-to-peer electronic cash system. To be fair, Nakamoto wasn't the first to float the idea. It is thought that whoever developed Bitcoin read *The Sovereign Individual*, a book published in 1997 forecasting that a new technology of money would decentralise and disintermediate the structure of society. The authors argued: *The Information Age implies another revolution in the character of money . . . This new form of money will reset the odds, reducing the capacity of the world's nation-states to determine who becomes a Sovereign Individual.* Proposing a form of *cybercash* that would be *unique, anonymous and verifiable* and able to *accommodate the largest transactions* as well as *be divisible into the tiniest fraction of value.* It would *be tradable at a keystroke in a multi trillion-dollar wholesale market without borders*[*].

After the initial, tepid reaction, Bitcoin moved from an idea to a genuine new currency at a fascinating speed. The

------

[*] Davidson, J.D. and Rees-Mogg, W., *The Sovereign Individual* (Macmillan, London, 1997).

evolution of money has taken centuries, and for a lot of that time it has been controlled by governments and Central Banks. Bitcoin decentralised money away from those powers to create an open-source, decentralised peer-to-peer network that is secured using cryptography and is constantly verifying the rules.

Of course, it started slowly. There was no infrastructure around Bitcoin, so buying and selling was down to hobbyists and technically minded enthusiasts. According to Alex Preda, a professor of professions, markets and technology at King's Business School in London, *Bitcoin was a fringe phenomenon confined to a subculture of software engineering and not a financial phenomenon*[*].

The first time Bitcoin was used in a 'real world' transaction is known as 'Bitcoin Pizza Day'. In May 2010, programmer, Laszlo Hanyecz, offered to pay 10,000 Bitcoin to anyone who would deliver two pizzas to him. Hanyecz later admitted, 'I wanted to do the pizza thing because, to me, it was free pizza. I mean, I coded this thing and mined Bitcoin and I felt like I was winning the internet that day.'

Nineteen-year-old student, Jeremy Sturdivant, delivered the pizzas worth around $40 and received his 10,000 Bitcoin. Sadly for Sturdivant, he didn't keep the Bitcoin[†]. If he had it would be worth around $330 *million* (December 2023), the most expensive pizza delivery ever recorded on the planet!

All monetary systems must have three characteristics to work. They need to be a unit of account, a way to store value and a means of exchange. Even though Hanyecz's pizzas are

---

[*] Ashmore, D., 'Bitcoin Price History 2009 to 2022', *Forbes* (2022).

[†] Sparks, H., 'Infamous Bitcoin pizza guy who squandered $365M haul has no regrets', *New York Post* (2021).

considered the first Bitcoin transaction, Sturdivant bought the pizzas from Papa John's with dollars and exchanged them for Bitcoin. As a unit of account and store of value Bitcoin has always been strong because of the security and scarcity of the currency. Bitcoin's bigger challenge was always being perceived as a means of exchange.

And that problem was largely solved by Mt. Gox. Originally a platform for exchanging collectable cards, it shifted focus to Bitcoin in 2010, becoming one of the first major Bitcoin exchanges. Exchanges like Mt. Gox facilitated the buying and selling of Bitcoin by acting as an intermediary, allowing people to trade Bitcoin and providing acceptable levels of liquidity.

It's fair to say that Bitcoin's growth was initially driven by its anonymity and perception as a store of value while investors became increasingly concerned that monetary policy was debasing fiat currency. But, as demand growth moved from slow to rapid, while supply continued to grow at a fixed, predictable rate, speculators were attracted to Bitcoin. And Mt. Gox and other exchange platforms certainly made that speculation easier.

At its peak, Mt. Gox was handling 70–80 per cent of Bitcoin trading volume and was onboarding more and more Bitcoin users. There had been a few glitches over the years but the fatal blow came in February 2014 when Mt. Gox was hacked and lost 850,000 Bitcoin. By this point Bitcoin wasn't the only cryptocurrency in town. Litecoin became the first competitor in October 2011 and others followed (PPC and XRP in 2012, DOGE and NXT in 2013, DASH in 2014 and ETH in 2015). Cryptocurrency was here to stay, but the collapse of Mt. Gox did spook the market and cryptocurrency experienced its first (but not last) 'crypto-winter'.

ICO Bubble

Like any disruptive technology or innovation, those who were only in cryptocurrency for the speculative upside, left. The true believers and enthusiasts who recognised that cryptocurrency was never going to disappear stayed and the space remained dynamic despite the marked drop in temperature.

The emergence of the Ethereum blockchain in 2015 was, however, a new pivot point, not just for cryptocurrency but for additional innovation (and speculation). Remember, Ethereum was programmable in a way that the Bitcoin blockchain was not. That created the capacity for smart contracts and people started to experiment with the creation of their own tokens. To a certain extent, Ethereum lowered the barriers to entry in crypto. Rather than programming a new blockchain from scratch, developers could leverage the Ethereum network and issue their own tokens on it. We will discuss tokens in more detail later, but for now you could consider tokens as units of value with a variety of purposes, such as acquiring a specific service, exercise governance rights or participating in the profits generated by a particular project. By 2017 just about every start-up or project was using tokens to secure funding for development and operations. In the off-chain world, start-ups would secure funding from venture capitalists in exchange for a percentage of the business. But an 'Initial Coin Offering' (ICO) sought to raise the money by selling a token or 'coin' to early investors in exchange for established cryptocurrencies like Bitcoin or ETH. ICOs were a deliberate play on the better-known business term 'Initial Public Offering' when a company goes public and lists on a stock exchange.

Ethereum lowered the barriers to entry in crypto.

Ethereum played a crucial role in the ICO boom as it provided a platform for creating and executing smart contracts, where the terms of the contract could be written into the code directly. This in turn allowed for the creation of custom tokens using the ERC-20 standard. ERC-20, proposed by Fabian Vogelsteller and Vitalik Buterin in late 2015 and later formalised by EIP-20, is a standard interface for fungible tokens on the Ethereum blockchain and is still widely used for creating and managing digital assets on the Ethereum platform.

In an ICO, a project or start-up creates a new token and sells a portion of it to investors during the initial sale. Investors usually pay for the tokens using established cryptocurrencies like Bitcoin or Ethereum. What was so attractive about tokens was that the issuer didn't need to give away a percentage of the business in exchange for the funding. They gave away what was, essentially, a made-up currency. On the other side, acquirers of such tokens included investors and, more often, speculators. They were willing to give up their BTC or ETH in the hope that the project would succeed, and the token would increase in value substantially.

On paper, it was a great idea and became very popular. For example, in mid-2017 a start-up called Tezos announced it would create 'a new decentralized blockchain that governs itself by establishing a true digital commonwealth'. It raised $232 million in a wildly successful ICO without any loss of equity. Instead, a new digital currency called TEZ was parcelled out to buyers[*].

---

[*] Irrera, A., Stecklow, S. and Hughes Neghaiwi, B., 'Backroom battle imperils $230 million cryptocurrency venture', Reuters (2017).

In a certain way, ICOs were democratising the access to venture capital. Anyone, even with a small sum, could participate in the launch of a new project. Unfortunately, mixing democratisation with money and speculation often attracts bad actors and too many dubious projects were pitched to unsophisticated investors and speculators, leading to what was considered a Wild West of ICOs.

At their peak, ICOs were raising billions and at lightning speed. Status.im, a browsing/messaging app, raised $100 million in under three hours. Brave, a browser start-up launched by former Mozilla CEO, Brendan Eich, raised $35 million in under thirty seconds[*]. The selective, Darwinian process of raising money from venture capitalists was turned upside down and speculators flooded in.

Speculation was based on a hope that the coin would take off and it could then be swapped out for a higher number of Bitcoin or ETH vs the ICO price, or that the token would end up having material value in and of itself. But very few did.

A relative lack of regulatory oversight, led to both opportunities and risks. Some projects were accused of being scams. Some like 'jokecoin' and 'uselesscoin' didn't even bother trying to hide that fact and they still raised hundreds of thousands of dollars[†].

Needless to say, the ICO bubble burst in 2018 when the market cap of all cryptocurrency and tokens fell by $700 billion, an 85 per cent drop from its peak[‡].

---

[*] Koetsier, J., 'ICO Bubble? Startups Are Raising Hundreds of Millions of Dollars Via Initial Coin Offerings', *Inc Magazine* (2017).

[†] Ibid.

[‡] Qureshi, H., 'The ICO Bubble Explained in Three Moments', Hackernoon (2019).

The ICO boom eventually subsided and regulatory scrutiny increased. Many ICO projects faced legal challenges and the industry witnessed a shift toward more regulated fundraising methods such as Security Token Offerings (STOs) and Initial Exchange Offerings (IEOs).

However, the ICO boom did play a pivotal role in shaping the cryptocurrency industry, providing a fundraising model for blockchain projects. It also highlighted the need for regulatory clarity, investor protection and responsible project development. As the industry matured, fundraising methods evolved and lessons learned from the ICO era contributed to a more sustainable and regulated approach to token offerings.

The Future of Cryptocurrency

Where there is innovation and advance there will always be speculation. Human beings have been speculating on investment opportunities for centuries.

The first financial bubble is thought to be the Tulip bubble in 17th-century Holland. Tulips were introduced to Europe from the Ottoman Empire in the late 16th century. Initially prized for their unique and vibrant colours, tulips became a status symbol among the wealthy. Due to a virus, some tulips developed visually striking patterns and these rare bulbs became highly desirable. Speculators entered the market driving the price of rare tulip bulbs on the Dutch exchange through the roof. Everyone got in on the action, including common citizens, in the hope to make money. The tulip market reached its peak in early 1637 and the bubble burst not long after, leading to a severe collapse in tulip prices.

Fast forward to the end of 2020 and beginning of 2021 and we can see another bubble – this time, Bitcoin and other cryptocurrencies. Bitcoin started the year slowly. Then the Covid pandemic hit around mid-March 2020. The global markets dropped sharply and Bitcoin wasn't spared, losing 50 per cent of its value in less than forty-eight hours. Once again, many suggested that this time Bitcoin was finished.

But, once again, Central Banks stepped in the world over. Unchecked stimulus during economic shutdown and low interest rates pushed investors back toward Bitcoin. Bitcoin's inbuilt scarcity was appealing in light of governments' penchant for just printing money at the first sign of trouble. Once more, fears were raised about the potential debasement of fiat currencies and rampant inflation. It was post-GFC all over again – only this time on steroids.

> Unchecked stimulus during economic shutdown and low interest rates pushed investors back toward Bitcoin.

A favourable macroeconomic environment, coupled with the fear of missing out (FOMO) on a rally fuelled the speculation again. Too many people bored at home during lockdown facilitated a further surge of retail investing. Trading platforms and apps, easily accessible on a phone, acted as an additional catalyst for unsophisticated investors. This time even some institutional investors got involved.

Markets rallied, and so did Bitcoin. By the end of 2020, one Bitcoin was worth $29,000 with a market cap of more than $539 billion. Governments kept printing money and Bitcoin hit $40,000 at the start of 2021, $50,000 in February

2021 and $60,000 in March 2021. It hit an all-time high of close to $69,000 in November 2021*.

As of December 2023, the global crypto market cap is $1.53 *trillion*. There are a staggering 8,863 different cryptocurrencies. That said, most of them will go nowhere and more than three-quarters of the entire crypto market cap is represented by the three largest currencies (Figure 5.1).

#	Name	Price	1h%	24h%	7d%	Market Cap	Volume (24h)	Circulating Supply	Last 7 days
1	Bitcoin BTC	$41,702.53	▲ 0.04%	▼ 0.43%	▲ 11.97%	$815,771,992,786	$28,063,278,605 673,488 BTC	19,561,693 BTC	
2	Ethereum ETH	$2,203.23	▲ 0.04%	▼ 1.28%	▲ 8.62%	$264,895,388,942	$11,918,393,019 5,415,092 ETH	120,230,296 ETH	
3	Tether USDt USDT	$0.9997	▲ 0.01%	▼ 0.07%	▲ 0.03%	$89,790,887,128	$58,480,813,349 58,478,542,163 USDT	89,814,116,890 USDT	

Figure 5.1: Top Three Cryptocurrencies by Market Cap December 2023

Cryptocurrency is a permanent addition to the financial system. For years, whenever there was a price drop, the media would lament about how it was all a flash in the pan or a con. As Thomas Stackpole in the *Harvard Business Review* puts it, every time there is a crypto bad news story, *skeptics rush to dismiss it as dead, railing that it was always a scam for nerds and crooks and was nothing more than a fringe curiosity pushed by techno-libertarians and people who hate banks*[†].

Cryptocurrency is a permanent addition to the financial system.

But by 2022 even the *Economist* was telling a different story: *Crypto's detractors have long argued that it is useless –*

---

*   Ashmore, D., 'Bitcoin Price History 2009 to 2022', *Forbes* (2022).
†   Stackpole, T., 'What Is Web3?', *Harvard Business Review* (2022).

unless you are a money-launderer or con-artist – and predicted its demise . . . In fact, the picture is rather different: a sorting process is underway, as the dodgiest parts of the crypto world are exposed, while the other bits prove more resilient[*].

With each failure or boom and bust cycle, the underlying technology just gets stronger. If the cryptocurrency is weak, it will fail. If the platform is weak, it will fail and what is left is more resilience and an even more robust financial system. Made more robust, not less, because of cryptocurrency.

If we look out into the future, maybe twenty to thirty years ahead, it's unlikely that Bitcoin will achieve what it set out to do: to end the need for banks. Central Banks will always have an important role to play in controlling the supply of capital to track the economy. We may disagree on the methods they use and the impact of the policies they enact, but the need to control supply is central to a healthy economy and a stable currency. For all the benefits of having clarity on the supply of money, the history of Bitcoin so far told us that an undesirable consequence of programmable supply is extreme volatility at times when demand swings. Being able to pull and push certain economic levers to influence the economy is an important tool and will remain important. A Central Bank can add liquidity or remove liquidity, and by doing so can steer the economy to a certain extent or can allow currencies to move relative to the value of other currencies, thus rebalancing the situation between one country and another. This probably won't change.

---

[*] 'The cryptocurrency sell-off has exposed those swimming naked', https://www.economist.com/leaders/2022/05/18/the-cryptocurrency-sell-off-has-exposed-those-swimming-naked, *The Economist* (2022).

But what will probably change is the move from a mix of digital and physical currency to just digital. In parts of the UK, payments are already made almost entirely digitally. In rural parts of Continental Europe, it's maybe 50/50 digital and physical cash. In the next ten years, maybe faster, we will only use digital currencies and the 50/50 split may end up representing centralised digital money and blockchain money. After all, Bitcoin transactions for everyday purchases have been around for more than ten years. A combination of factors allowed the development of the so-called 'Bitcoin Valley' in a wealthy and well-banked area of northern Italy, in the Trentino Alto Adige region. In this Bitcoin Valley, local merchants started accepting Bitcoin as a form of payment in 2013. Even more interesting is the broad adoption of Bitcoin payments through the community and the wide range of businesses accepting it, from wine bars to butcher shops and even golf clubs and hotels*.

Another phenomenon may take place in the next decades: the well-established cryptocurrencies such as Bitcoin and ETH will likely be joined by Central Bank Digital Currencies (CBDCs). And money will flow both on and off-chain. This will happen off-chain in much the same way as it's possible today, by tapping your card or using your phone or an app. At the same time and in parallel, transactions made on the blockchain will allow for instant settlement from one person's digital wallet to another. This is not possible with the current infrastructure and not possible without the blockchain. And this will also be possible between countries and currencies

---

* Mehilli, L., 'An Empirical Study on the Adoption of Cryptocurrency E-Payment Systems in Italian Business Platforms', (2018) http://dspace.unive.it/bitstream/handle/10579/12959/837734-1201433.pdf

making transactions easier, faster and cheaper than current standards. For decades, if you lived in the US and wanted to send money back to your sister in the Philippines, the process was slow, painful and expensive because there are several companies between your account and your sister's account. And each company or party takes a fee. But, in the future, these transfers will be instant on-chain and wallet to wallet, with no third-party intervention and very little fees. Your sister in Manila will receive digital currency in a matter of seconds and will be able to spend it at local merchants instantaneously.

The well-established cryptocurrencies such as Bitcoin and ETH will likely be joined by Central Bank Digital Currencies (CBDCs).

The costs incurred today by millions of migrants that want to send money back home would be reduced to virtually zero, with a wallet-to-wallet transfer happening on-chain in seconds or even milliseconds. If we combine fintech with digital currencies, we can imagine a future where a migrant in America can access an early wage advance service sending money to the other side of the world before they've even been paid their salary. This would happen seamlessly through a fintech app that allows the user to spend their money as they earn it, even before it is paid out by the employer. All of this is already feasible today. The 'rail tracks', so to speak, have already been laid. It is just a matter of integrating different products and services through more user-friendly interfaces to allow adoption to gradually increase.

In some cases, the very low marginal cost of any transaction is already allowing the evolution of new forms of payments such as 'streaming payments'. Instant settlements and low marginal costs on certain blockchains make it possible to execute a series of microtransactions at very short intervals, thus making it possible to effectively make a payment for every second or minute of use of a certain service in real time. There could be many useful applications, including a pay-as-you-go system for car insurance. In this case, a car could send a signal every time it was started to its insurance company. Insurance could be paid in real time by the second and, technically speaking, AI algorithms could also judge the quality of driving to adjust the risk-based element of the insurance premium in real time. Video streaming subscriptions could also benefit from streaming payments. Consider participation in an expensive online webinar. A potential customer may be reluctant to participate due to the high cost and being unsure if it will be of any value. Streaming payments could allow more customers to take the risk and assess the usefulness in real time. If not useful, you could disconnect, and the flow of payments stops right there. As usual, once the innovation becomes more popular, new use cases would pop up every day.

Digital currencies may also make a more transparent world, where all transactions are recorded on the blockchain and are traceable. This characteristic, combined with wallet identification and enhanced privacy feature, could represent a major step in tackling crime and money laundering.

We may reach a point in the future when a baby automatically gets a digital wallet at birth. This wallet is encrypted and NFTs will be added over time for all the documents (national ID, passport, driving licence, etc.) alongside digital currency. Every transaction that person makes will pass through this wallet. They would not need a bank account anymore. Know Your Customer (KYC) protocols would be seamless and instantaneous, as those NFTs representing the digital identity of a person would be easily accessible and verifiable by third parties. When that person grows up and starts working, their salary would be paid into the wallet. To us right now, this idea might sound dystopian, as we worry about privacy. But there is already a significant sharing of information and blockchain would provide greater privacy not less. Let's not forget that, today, certain entities already have access. Police, for example, can get a warrant to access all the transactions we make on our credit card and have access to all our personal data too. In addition, hackers may be able to obtain the same information illegally and that information may even include our credit card number. In that context, the idea of having an alphanumeric wallet assigned for all our transactions may not necessarily sound like a very invasive idea, especially if access to the information connecting an individual to a wallet could only be provided under legally enforced authority such as during a money laundering investigation.

Of course, the transition from our current centralised financial system to full or partially decentralised finance will not happen overnight. It's like the transition from physical letters to email. Initially people didn't like email and were not sure if they could trust it, but today email is ubiquitous. Email too may end up being phased out over time in favour of systems like Slack or WhatsApp, but the way we communicate has always evolved and will continue to evolve. The same is true of money and our use of money. It took many decades for electronic money to take over cash. This process was certainly accelerated during the global pandemic as people stopped using cash for fear of catching the virus from the physical money. We can expect a similarly long journey for digital currencies to become ubiquitous but it will happen and they will make our lives easier and safer.

Digital Tokens and Tokenisation

The ICO bubble was driven by speculation and, whilst that bubble burst, the underlying concept of a coin or token to indicate ownership and potentially a store of value had proven itself to be a very useful model.

The terminology around tokens and cryptocurrencies can be quite confusing; they are sometimes used interchangeably, but they are different. Cryptocurrencies like Bitcoin (BTC), Ethereum (ETH) and Litecoin (LTC) operate on their own independent blockchains. Tokens represent native assets of a specific blockchain network and they typically serve as a medium of exchange, store of value and unit of account within their respective blockchain networks and typically for specific projects. Tokens are created ('minted') and distributed through a process called a token sale or initial coin offering (ICO) on a blockchain like Ethereum. They can represent various assets, such as real-world assets, ownership in a project, governance rights or access to a particular application or service. Tokens can be fungible (such as ERC-20 tokens on the Ethereum network) or non-fungible (NFTs), which represent unique, indivisible assets like digital art or collectibles.

Cryptocurrencies are therefore native to their own blockchain networks and serve as a form of digital currency, while tokens are built on existing blockchain platforms and can represent a variety of assets and functionalities beyond simple currency.

It is these additional functionalities that are proving so potent.

Asset Tokenisation

Because the building block innovations around digital assets such as blockchain emerged from the field of data science, many of the terms we now use to describe capabilities are taken from those fields. The term *token* is a good example. In data science a token is a value, like a randomly generated number, assigned to sensitive data to mask the original information. And in a blockchain, a token is a number assigned to data stored within the blockchain. Giving an asset a token is called 'tokenisation'[*].

And it is tokenisation that makes these additional functionalities possible. Tokenisation refers to the process of converting rights to an asset into a digital token on a blockchain using smart contracts. This process can be applied to various types of assets, including real estate, stocks, bonds and even tangible assets like art or commodities.

> Tokenisation refers to the process of converting rights to an asset into a digital token on a blockchain using smart contracts.

Until the building block innovations of blockchain, DLTs, smart contracts and DApps emerged, ownership of assets was largely a paper-based off-line/off-chain process with various intermediaries involved to negotiate and execute

---

[*] Majaski, C. and Anderson, S., 'Cryptocurrency Security Token: Definition, Forms, Investing In', Investopedia (2022).

a transaction. The nature of these transactions always meant that sometimes the transaction would not go ahead, as one of the parties would pull out of the deal. All the intermediaries such as agents and lawyers knew this so they would automatically bake extra costs into the system as compensation. But with the blockchain and smart contracts the trust variable is removed because the intermediaries are removed. The moment a smart contract is executed on the blockchain, the will of the two parties becomes irrelevant: if A happens, then B will be executed. If A does not happen then B will not be executed. It is defined, it is permanent and can't be tampered with. Such characteristics add tremendous value as they solve problems that have always been extremely difficult to mitigate in the traditional world.

Tokenisation brings traditional assets onto blockchain platforms, offering a wide range of benefits including increased liquidity, instant settlement, fractional ownership, enhanced security, transparency and compliance, efficiency, and reduced costs. More people are in the market for the asset and exchanges may be established to facilitate the matching of supply and demand, which increases liquidity. More people have access to ownership and investment opportunities that would have been out of their reach before tokenisation. And, as the asset is recorded on the blockchain, it is far more secure than a paper-based system or even an encrypted digital system.

> Tokenisation brings traditional assets onto blockchain platforms, offering a wide range of benefits.

Asset tokenisation leverages blockchain technology to enhance liquidity, increase accessibility, improve security and streamline financial processes. These benefits have the potential to revolutionise traditional asset markets, making them more efficient, inclusive and secure, while also offering new investment opportunities to a broader range of participants.

The process of tokenisation may involve, as an example, the creation of digital tokens that are legally linked to the ownership of a digital or a real-world asset. The transactions associated with those tokens are then recorded on a blockchain, providing transparency, traceability, and security around the ownership and transfer of these assets. However, tokens can have various characteristics and serve different purposes including security tokens, utility tokens, asset-backed tokens and NFTs.

Security Tokens

A security token represents ownership or investment in a tradable financial asset, company, equity, debt, profit-sharing rights or other financial instruments.

The key characteristic of security tokens is that they grant investors certain rights or entitlements related to the financial performance of the underlying asset or the issuing entity. And, because they represent ownership or investment in a tradable financial asset, they are subject to securities regulations and fall under the supervision of the SEC and other regulatory bodies. This is currently a significant hindrance to their advance and utilisation due to the complexity and limitations associated with securities law, but, on the positive side, regulation helps address many of the issues witnessed during the ICO bubble of 2017.

The key characteristic of security tokens is that they grant investors certain rights or entitlements related to the financial performance of the underlying asset or the issuing entity.

That said, security tokens still offer several use cases, primarily centred around representing ownership or investment in traditional financial assets in a more efficient and accessible manner.

Common uses include:

- **Equity Ownership:** Security tokens can represent ownership in a company, giving investors equity in the form of tokenised shares. This allows for more efficient and transparent ownership tracking on a blockchain.
- **Debt Instruments:** Security tokens can be used to represent ownership of debt instruments, such as bonds. Tokenisation streamlines the issuance, trading, settlement and management of debt securities, potentially reducing costs and increasing liquidity.
- **Venture Capital and Start-ups:** Security tokens can be issued by start-ups and companies seeking venture capital. This provides investors with tokenised ownership stakes in the company and it allows for more streamlined and programmable compliance with regulations.
- **Tokenised Fund:** Security tokens can represent ownership in investment funds, providing investors with exposure to diversified portfolios of assets. This tokenisation of funds can simplify the management and transfer of fund shares.
- **Dividend Distribution:** Security tokens can automate the distribution of dividends and profit-sharing. Smart contracts can be programmed to automatically

THE FUTURE OF FINANCE

distribute earnings to token holders in a transparent
and auditable manner.

- **Governance and Voting:** Security tokens can be designed to
  confer voting rights in the governance of a project
  or company. Token holders may participate in
  decision-making processes related to the direction and
  development of the entity.

Security tokens aim to provide more liquidity, transparency
and efficiency in traditional financial markets by leveraging
blockchain technology.

We can expect several trends influencing security tokens
in the future.

First, we are going to see more use of security tokens.
As previously mentioned, the cryptocurrency market is
worth approximately \$1.53 trillion dollars. Many well-
established asset managers are already tapping into this
wealth base with digital twins of real-world financial assets
such as treasury bonds and investment funds. A digital twin
is a virtual representation or model of a physical object,
system or process. It is a digital counterpart that mirrors
the characteristics, behaviour and status of its real-world
counterpart in real time.

While the use of digital twins is in the early days of
experimentation, we may see an increasing degree of
sophistication in the offers and a broader on-chain financial
market. In the not so distant future, investors could be able
to buy shares on an S&P 500 company on the stock exchange
or on a blockchain.

Second, there may be an evolution of the regulatory
landscape. As previously mentioned, although regulation is
fundamental to tackle bad actors, it represents significant

friction to the distribution of security tokens and a substantial barrier to entry for early-stage ventures. The debate between investor protection and freedom to access a broader range of financial opportunities will intensify and could lead to surprising outcomes. As an example, when our entire personal wealth is held 'on chain', certain tokens could be acquired by a wallet only up to a specific percentage of the overall assets, thus protecting investors from excessive losses or risk concentration. Or a smart contract, analysing all past transactions of a wallet, may issue a financial literacy certificate that may allow the access to certain tokens.

Finally, we are probably going to see increased democratisation in the offering of products that for decades have only been accessible to the wealthiest clients. Tokens allow fractionalisation, and this will change investments in certain asset classes forever. Since the beginning, art as a form of investment has only been available to the super wealthy. To match the purchase price of even the cheapest Picasso painting ever sold you would need $118 million[*]. Today, such paintings can be tokenised and fractionalised. Retail investors may acquire a tiny fraction of the work of art, represented by a token. They could vote, through their token, on whether they want to lend the painting to a museum or put it up for auction. They could share in the profits or sell their fractions on the secondary market to willing buyers. We can expect an entire ecosystem of players entering this market, providing tokenisation and fractionalisation services, creating exchanges that offer liquidity and transaction

---

[*] Mullennix, B., 'What Are The Cheapest Picasso Paintings (Revealed!)', Artistry Found.

capabilities and advisory services to guide investors through the process. Imagine the impact of a secondary market on tokenised art on the elite auction house industry, who have benefited from 20 per cent or more commissions on sales for decades.

Utility Tokens

Whereas security tokens represent ownership in underlying assets and are subject to securities regulations, offering ownership rights and potential financial returns, utility tokens provide access to specific services or products within blockchain ecosystems and do not convey ownership rights, serving functional purposes within decentralised applications and platforms. A utility token is a type of digital asset that is issued to fundraise for a specific project and is intended to provide access to a particular product or service within a blockchain ecosystem, decentralised application (DApp) or platform.

It is not always easy to differentiate between a utility token and a security token, and regulators are trying to find a common standard to define it. For example, the US Securities and Exchange Commission (SEC) considers certain tokens as securities based on the 'Howey Test', a legal framework established by the US Supreme Court in the case of SEC v. W.J. Howey Co. (1946). The Howey Test is used to determine whether an investment contract qualifies as a security and is subject to securities regulations. Here are the key criteria of the Howey Test and how they might apply to some tokens:

- **Investment of Money:** This criterion is met when individuals invest money with the expectation of earning a profit. In the context of token sales or initial coin offerings (ICOs), individuals typically purchase tokens using fiat currency or cryptocurrencies, effectively meeting this requirement.
- **Common Enterprise:** A common enterprise is present when investors' fortunes are interlinked or pooled with those of the token issuer or a third party. In many ICOs or token offerings, funds raised from investors are used to develop and promote a project or platform. The success of the project often affects the value of the tokens, creating a common enterprise.
- **Expectation of Profit:** Investors must have a reasonable expectation of profit primarily from the efforts of others, typically the efforts of the token issuer or a third party. If investors anticipate that the actions of the issuer or a specific team will lead to an increase in token value, this criterion is satisfied.
- **Efforts of Others:** This aspect emphasises that the profit expectation should be dependent on the efforts of the token issuer or a third party rather than the investor's own actions. If the development, marketing or management of the project is primarily undertaken by the issuer or a third party, this condition is met.

It was utility tokens that caused the ICO bubble. Essentially all these companies issued their own coin or utility token that allowed users to utilise them in the network or exchange them for another cryptocurrency.

It was utility tokens that caused the ICO bubble.

Say, for example, one of those companies was a business that needed funding to expand a chain of pizzas. You might like pizza so you decide to invest $2,000 worth of Bitcoin and receive 5,000 PizzaCoins, the idea being that you would then use those PizzaCoins to buy pizza, therefore recouping your investment and helping the business to succeed at the same time. But what if your 5,000 PizzaCoins were suddenly worth $10,000? You would sell them and you wouldn't buy the pizza. If everyone did that, the PizzaCoin value would collapse because of the mismatch between supply and demand, at which point buyers would once again jump in as the price of pizza in PizzaCoins becomes too cheap. The whole process would normally lead to equilibrium. But what if speculators push the price of PizzaCoin to unsustainable levels or if the product, rather than being pizza, was something nobody really wanted? This is exactly what happened in the ICO bubble. People bought utility tokens even when they didn't intend to utilise them in the network and the underlying product had scarce demand; they would instead simply watch the price movements trying to buy low and sell high – in a nutshell, speculate. It was this huge volatility and limited connection to the intrinsic value of a token that ultimately caused the ICO bubble to burst.

Intrinsically, utility tokens serve various use cases within blockchain ecosystems and decentralised applications (DApps). Common uses include:

- **Access to Platform Service:** One of the primary use cases for utility tokens is to provide access to specific services or features within a blockchain platform or decentralised application. Users need these tokens to utilise the functionalities offered by the platform. As an example, a blockchain-based software platform could raise funds by offering tokens that could be used to unlock some specific functionalities or perform activities.

- **Transaction Fees:** Utility tokens can be used to pay for transaction fees within a blockchain network. For example, when users perform transactions or execute smart contracts, they may be required to use utility tokens to cover the associated costs.

- **Incentive Programs:** Utility tokens can be used to create incentive structures within a blockchain ecosystem. Projects may reward users with tokens for contributing to the growth of the network by inviting others, participating in governance or engaging in specific activities that benefit the overall ecosystem.

- **Voting Rights in Governance:** Some utility tokens confer voting rights, allowing holders to participate in the governance and decision-making processes of the blockchain project. This democratic approach involves token holders in key decisions related to upgrades, changes or other aspects of the project's development.

- **Staking and Consensus Mechanisms:** Utility tokens are often used in consensus mechanisms where token holders 'stake' their tokens to support network security, validate transactions and potentially earn rewards in the form of additional tokens.

- **Access to Exclusive Content:** In some decentralised applications, utility tokens are required to access premium or exclusive content. This model is common in content-sharing platforms, where users can use tokens to unlock special features or content.

- **Identity and Access Management:** Utility tokens can be utilised in decentralised identity systems, where they serve as a means of proving identity or granting access to certain resources or services.

Utility tokens are versatile and can be customised to fit the specific needs of a blockchain project using smart contracts. The key is to align the utility of the token with the functionality and purpose of the decentralised platform or application it represents. For example, if we have a blockchain-based software platform for customer relationships, the logical function of a token may be the ability to add records to your database, while maybe receiving voting rights on the project would not appear as attractive. At the other end of the spectrum, if Wikipedia was on-chain, participants may be more interested in having tokens to influence the governance and direction of the project, and the tokens may be distributed as a form of incentive program to participate in the growth of the knowledge base.

Looking to the future, we can expect years and decades of endless experimentation. We have just started scratching the surface of what is possible through utility tokens and, as usual, creativity will do the rest. In finance, utility tokens will play a major role in two ways:

- By linking tokens to the future use of a product or service, companies – especially those with niche products that cater to a base of very active supporters – may find new ways to raise financial capital. The concept is not dissimilar to the pre-sale of properties in a real estate development. In very much the same way, certain supporters of a new product may be willing to pay for tokens that will give them early or exclusive access to it in the future.

- By offering tokens as a form of incentive, companies will be able to launch and develop initiatives with the willing contributions of third parties. From simple 'refer a friend' token programs to attribution of tokens in proportion to contributions, businesses will be able to tap into the desire of people to become part of something. In this case, the financial angle is more subtle and more linked to the reduced amount of capital required when launching a project thanks to the issuance of incentive tokens.

> Looking to the future, we can expect years and decades of endless experimentation.

Asset-backed Tokens

Asset-backed tokens are a subset of security tokens and represent ownership or a claim on a specific real-world asset. The value of the token is pegged to the value of the underlying asset. These assets can include commodities (such as gold or silver), real estate or other tangible assets.

The primary purpose of asset-backed tokens is to provide a digital representation of ownership in a physical asset and, as explained for security tokens, they may offer benefits such as increased liquidity and fractional ownership. This type of tokenisation of real-world assets (RWA) is a great use case of the bridge that is being created between fintech and the blockchain, and it represents a significant leap in linking the blockchain universe to the real economy.

The primary purpose of asset-backed tokens is to provide a
digital representation of ownership in a physical asset.

This fusion addresses a crucial challenge: connecting the
often abstract, digital world of blockchain with tangible,
real-world assets. By tokenising RWAs, we are creating a
direct link between the blockchain and the real operating
economy, involving actual consumers and users and physical
goods and services. This connection is pivotal because it
extends the benefits of blockchain – such as transparency,
security and efficiency – to a broader range of assets and
economic activities. In fact, while a lot of security tokens
simply create digital twins of already available financial
products, asset-backed tokens can be native on-chain.
This means that the underlying financial product does not
necessarily exist in a traditional finance setting but is created
for the first time directly on the blockchain through a smart
contract. Loans to individuals and SMEs can be issued as
NFTs and those NFTs, with the associated contractual cash
flows, can be grouped in a larger pool in a process called
securitisation.

Securitisation is nothing new; it has been around for
decades. In essence, the process of securitisation involves
the grouping of many loans in a single, marketable security,
whose value is backed by the value (and the cash flows) of all
the underlying loans. As long as securitisation is not abused
(such as during the GFC), it is a powerful instrument that
allows a more efficient solution for the funding of real loans
to the real economy.

A lot of experimentation in this field has already taken
place in the past few years, with several crypto start-ups
proposing on-chain versions of securitisations. In the

fertile world of start-ups, tokenisation of real-world assets is probably the area where fintech companies and crypto businesses have found the best opportunity to cooperate. Fintech lenders have strong origination capabilities for niche products in underserved markets, while crypto firms have the technology to tokenise those products and distribute them to a crypto investor base.

By tokenising RWAs, we are creating a direct link between the blockchain and the real operating economy.

Asset-backed tokens facilitate a better alignment of the digital financial services with the needs and realities of the real economy, ensuring that the advancements in technology are not just theoretical but have a practical and beneficial impact on everyday economic activities.

The tokenisation of RWAs stands as a testament to the potential of blockchain and fintech to revolutionise the financial industry and have a positive, tangible impact on the broader, real-world economy. And this synergy is also a pathway to more inclusive and diversified economic participation.

Tokenisation of Real-World Assets (RWAs) through Asset-backed Tokens is therefore considered one of the most promising and transformative use cases for blockchain technology and fintech in the financial industry. Take tangible assets like real estate, artwork or traditional securities and convert them into digital tokens that can be securely and transparently traded on blockchain platforms. While the idea itself is not new, the advent of blockchain technology has brought unprecedented efficiency, transparency and accessibility to this process.

It allows unlocking liquidity in illiquid assets, by breaking down these assets into smaller, tradable units, effectively fractionalising them. It brings with it democratisation of investment opportunities as it allows individuals from various walks of life to participate in assets previously reserved for the privileged few. Imagine owning a fraction of a historic landmark or a stake in a thriving start-up. This newfound inclusivity empowers a wider population to engage in asset markets, potentially reducing wealth disparities. Tokenisation, combined with the blockchain's immutable ledger, allows for a transparent and tamper-resistant record of ownership and transactions, with universal access and reduced counterparty credit risks. The automation of asset management processes, reduction of intermediaries, and elimination of manual paperwork translate into substantial cost savings for both issuers and investors. Furthermore, Asset-backed Tokens create secondary markets for traditionally illiquid assets, providing investors with exit opportunities and mechanisms for price discovery.

> Tokenisation allows for a transparent and tamper-resistant record of ownership and transactions, with universal access and reduced counterparty credit risks.

The tokenisation of real-world assets through Asset-backed Tokens is not merely a technological advancement; it represents a fundamental shift in how we perceive, access and trade assets. However, it is crucial to acknowledge that regulatory challenges, security considerations and tech-nological hurdles remain on the path to full realisation of these benefits. Yet, as blockchain technology continues to mature and regulatory frameworks adapt, the promise of

Asset-backed Tokens remains a beacon of transformation in the financial world – a potential game-changer that empowers individuals and reshapes markets.

NFTs

NFT stands for 'Non-Fungible Token'. It is a type of digital asset that represents ownership or proof of authenticity of a unique item or piece of content using blockchain technology.

The first known NFT was created in 2014 by Kevin McCoy and Anil Dash. Registered on the Namecoin blockchain, 'Quantum' consisted of a short video clip and became the first example of a 'monetised graphic'. Initially, McCoy sold it to Dash for $4. A version of that original NFT was sold by Sotheby's in 2021 for $1.4 million[*]. Needless to say, NFTs, like cryptocurrency, have attracted speculators.

The two big names in NFTs are Pak and Beeple. In January 2021 Beeple, whose real name is Mike Winkelmann, created an NFT called *Everydays: The First 5,000 Days*, a digital collage that consists of 5,000 individual images created by the artist every day over the span of 5,000 days (over thirteen years). It was sold by Christie's auction house in March 2021 for a staggering $69.3 million. In 2022 Beeple sold another NFT, this one called *Human One*, the world's first physical sculpture that evolves over time. It was sold for $28.9 million.

In February 2022 Pak, real identity unknown, collaborated with Julian Assange to create an NFT called *Clock*. The

---

[*]   Di Liscia, V., '"First Ever NFT" Sells for $1.4 Million', Hyperallergic (2021).

artwork is a simple counter that shows the number of days Julian Assange, founder of WikiLeaks, has been imprisoned. The digital asset was purchased by AssangeDAO, a group of over 10,000 Assange supporters, for $52.7 million (more on DAOs in a moment). Pak also currently holds the NFT record for a collection of digital artworks called *The Merge*, which sold for a mind-blowing $91.8 million in December 2021[*].

The size of the market has varied wildly with the speculation which peaked in 2021, probably fuelled by the same boredom during lockdown that saw so many people dabble in cryptocurrency and the stock market. In 2021, the digital art NFT market, which has been around less than a decade, ballooned to $41 billion. This is extraordinary considering that the conventional art market, which has been around for centuries, was worth about $50 billion in the same year[†].

Key characteristics of NFTs include:

- **Uniqueness:** Each NFT is distinct and has unique information that sets it apart from other tokens. This uniqueness is often associated with digital or digitised assets like art, collectibles or virtual items in games.
- **Ownership and Authenticity:** NFTs are stored on a blockchain, providing a transparent and verifiable record of ownership. The blockchain serves as a

---

[*] No Author, 'Top Highest Selling NFTs in 2022 October That You Should Be Aware Of!', ForexBrokerReview (2022).

[†] Dailey, N.,'NFTs ballooned to a $41 billion market in 2021 and are catching up to the total size of the global fine art market', Markets Insider (2022).

decentralised ledger that certifies the authenticity and ownership history of the digital asset.

- **Indivisibility:** NFTs cannot be divided into smaller units like traditional cryptocurrencies. They exist as whole tokens, reinforcing the idea of owning a complete and unique item.
- **Interoperability:** Many NFTs are built on standards such as ERC-721 (Ethereum) or ERC-1155, allowing for interoperability of exchange and functionality across different platforms and marketplaces.
- **Smart Contracts:** NFTs often utilise smart contracts to encode specific rules or functionalities. Smart contracts can include details about royalties for creators, ensuring they receive a percentage of future sales when the NFT is resold.

NFTs have gained widespread popularity in various creative industries, including digital art, music, virtual real estate and gaming. Artists, musicians and content creators can tokenise their work, allowing them to sell and monetise digital assets in a way that was not easily achievable before blockchain technology.

As an example, let's consider prospects for a famous musician. An NFT could be created of a particular live rendition of a song. This NFT could be auctioned off to a fan, who would be the exclusive owner of that particular digital file. The smart contract of the NFT could allow the owner to resell or license the song according to predefined criteria and royalties could flow automatically to the wallets of the artist, her manager, and the owner of the song. NFTs, just like security or utility tokens, could become crucial forms of financing in the future.

And they are not just for the speculators or the computer engineers; businesses are taking note. Many NFTs are offering companies with physical real-world products a way into a new, flourishing digital marketplace. The initial examples have represented a natural evolution of the original function of NFTs, representing digital artwork.

In 2021 Nike bought RTFKT, a digital design studio producing trainers and other collectibles that can be worn across different online environments. In April the following year, Nike revealed their debut digital trainers, Nike Cryptokicks, customisable with eight skins made by RTFKT's community of artists and collaborators*. Adidas sold $23 million worth of NFTs in less than a day and instantly created a resale market on OpenSea (a sort of eBay for NFTs)†.

Founded in 1909, L'Oréal Group created seventeen NFT product lines and registered several digital trademarks for its most well-known beauty brands, indicating that it intends to enter the virtual cosmetics market. L'Oréal already owns a virtual shop in Decentraland, a virtual reality platform built on blockchain technology, allowing users to create, explore and monetise content and applications in a decentralised, user-owned virtual world‡.

Tokenisation, along with the building blocks of blockchain, (DLTs, smart contracts and DApps) plays a crucial role in the Decentraland ecosystem, providing ownership and representation of virtual assets within the platform.

---

* Lim, J., 'Nike and RTFKT unveil virtual trainers NFT', theindustry. fashion (2022).
† Stackpole, T., 'What is Web3?', *Harvard Business Review* (2022).
‡ Cox, D., 'L'Oréal Prioritizes NFTs and the Metaverse', CryptoNewsZ (2022).

In March 2022, some of the biggest names in fashion including Estee Lauder, DKNY, Dolce & Gabbana, Tommy Hilfiger, Karl Lagerfeld and *Vogue* participated in the first ever large-scale virtual Metaverse Fashion Week in Decentraland[*]. Estee Lauder unveiled its first wearable NFT, where users were able to step virtually inside the Advanced Night Repair 'Little Brown Bottle' to unlock a digital token and claim one NFT wearable giving the user's avatar a radiant aura inspired by their Advanced Night Repair product[†].

And in January 2023, L'Oréal's corporate venture capital fund BOLD (Business Opportunities for L'Oréal Development) invested in US-based start-up, Digital Village, a metaverse-as-a-service platform and NFT marketplace for brands, creators and communities, signalling once again how seriously they take the digital marketplace[‡]. Banks too are getting in on the action. In early 2022 J.P. Morgan Onyx, the bank's blockchain unit, opened a 'lounge' in the Decentraland Metaverse[§].

It is tokenisation together with the building blocks of digital assets that are making these virtual marketplaces possible.

In Decentraland for example, there are three main tokens: MANA, LAND and wearables. MANA, an ERC-20 token

---

[*] No Author, 'Fashion takes center-stage in the Metaverse at Decentraland's Metaverse Fashion Week', GlobalNewsWire (2023).

[†] Sternberg, C., 'Beauty in the Metaverse: What Is It and Why are Beauty Companies Investing in It?', Beautypacking.com (2023).

[‡] Ibid.

[§] Shevlin, R., 'J.P. Morgan Opens A Bank Branch In The Metaverse (But It's Not What You Think It's For)', *Forbes* (2022).

on the Ethereum blockchain, acts as the native currency in Decentraland. Users can buy and sell virtual land, goods and services in the platform using MANA. In May 2022, part of the Singapore-based Millennium Hotels brand opened the world's first virtual hotel in Decentraland[*]. The Digital Fashion Week mentioned earlier was hosted by Metaverse Group in an area of virtual real estate they bought in late 2021 for a record-breaking $2.43 million[†]. Remember this is not physical land or buildings – it's virtual. LAND, as the name would suggest, is an ERC-721 token that represents the virtual plot. Each parcel of virtual land is an individual non-fungible token (NFT) with a unique identifier. And, finally, the wearable tokens are used to buy, sell and wear virtual items known as 'wearables'. Each wearable is an ERC-721 token, making it unique and tradable.

Tokenisation within Decentraland and beyond is fundamental to representing ownership of virtual assets, facilitating transactions and enabling the decentralised governance of the platform. The use of blockchain and NFTs ensures transparency, security and interoperability within the virtual world, allowing users to truly own and trade their digital assets on a decentralised platform.

It is fair to say that most of what we have seen so far is early days experimentation. To many, the Decentraland metaverse is a new version of something already seen before – does anyone remember the launch of Second Life in 2003? Second Life was an early days Metaverse created by Linden

---

[*] Thackray, L., 'First "Virtual Hotel" opens in the Metaverse', *Independent* (2022).

[†] Graves, S., 'Decentraland Virtual Land Plot sells for Record $2.43 million', Decrypt.co (2021).

Labs. People could buy land, build virtual businesses and sell virtual items. The main difference is that – at the time – these were not NFTs and the platform was not decentralised. If Linden Labs failed, the whole project failed. But this did not discourage users from all over the world and, almost fifteen years after the frenzy started, Second Life's economy still had a GDP of approximately $500 million dollars, according to its CEO[*]. As you can see, the examples reported above are not dissimilar to what happened in the late 1990s or early 2000s with the launch of the World Wide Web. A new technology was born and there was a frenzy of activity to experiment with new business models and ideas, often unrealistic, sometimes even delusional. But from this highly creative period, new business models were born that changed the world over the following decades.

If we concentrate on the key underlying characteristics of NFTs, we can move away from some of the initial use cases (such as digital art) and we could investigate applications of real-world value.

Gaming is a fascinating example, with interesting connections and overlaps with finance. In what has been the most popular crypto game, Axie Infinity[†], players buy, collect, breed and battle with little pets called Axies. Each pet has unique characteristics, defined by an algorithm, and is a tradable NFT. At its peak, Axie Infinity had over 2.7 million daily users. What's interesting is that the popularity of the project led to the creation of its own economy. Gamers were battling to gain tokens, which could be sold for established

---

[*] Miaberg, E., 'Why Is "Second Life" Still a Thing?' Motherboard Tech by Vice (2016).
[†] 'Axie Infinity', Wikipedia [accessed January 2024].

cryptocurrencies. Hence, more powerful Axies were worth a lot for their token acquisition capabilities. Soon, wealthier players started renting powerful Axies to players with less money but more available free time to play and an economy was born. In crypto games, promoters can fund the business with an initial offer of NFTs to early adopters and later take a cut from the emergence of the underlying game economy. Unlike traditional video games, where 100 per cent of the proceeds of all the purchases go to the developer, in crypto games users can earn money.

If we move to the core of finance, we can also expect an increasing number of applications for NFTs. Their uniqueness and authenticity make them a useful technology for storing and providing personal ID information. Know your client (KYC) and anti-money laundering (AML) checks, currently representing a cumbersome but mandatory task for the onboarding of new clients, may be streamlined in the future if a common standard can be agreed, a future where each person has a personal digital wallet with NFT-ed IDs, could allow instantaneous KYC checks.

> If we move to the core of finance, we can also expect an increasing number of applications for NFTs.

Other interesting applications could revolutionise invoice financing. In Europe, invoice financing, the process of obtaining finance secured by invoices payable by a company's client, represents a 2 trillion Euro market. However, billions are lost every year due to fraud, such as when bad actors sell the same invoice to two or more debt providers at the same time. In a future where all invoices will be issued on a blockchain as NFTs, duplicates will not be financeable and the cash flow from repayments could be handled through smart contracts, allowing for more security. A safer invoice financing market with a lower incidence of fraud cases will lead to lower risk investment opportunities and, as a result of this positive feedback loop, lower cost of funding.

Funding, Ownership and Governance Changes

Although we have covered the varied uses of tokens, and how these are specifically designed to facilitate funding and ownership and improve governance, it is easy to miss these capabilities amongst all the varied things that tokens and tokenisation can achieve. It is therefore worth drawing attention to how digital tokens, usually security or utility tokens, will play a major role in the funding of new economic initiatives as well as managing ownership and governance.

Let's consider the launch of a social network platform like Facebook, but twenty years from now. Remember Metcalfe's Law? Metcalfe's Law states that the value of a network is proportional to the square of the number of connected users of the system[*]. In other words, every time you add a new participant to the network, they don't just slightly increase the effectiveness of the network, they square the effectiveness of the whole network. A Facebook of the future would almost certainly incentivise users to join by issuing tokens while still retaining part of the value as a promoter. Not only that, all the future activity on the network, such as posting a video, inviting a friend, leaving a comment could lead to

---

[*]   Naughton, J., 'For the first time in its history, Facebook is in decline. Has the tech giant begun to crumble?', *Guardian* (2022).

the distribution of additional tokens. Even the access to our own data used by an advertiser can be monetised through tokens, with a small part attributed to the users themselves.

Tokens, in a nutshell, provide a system of economic incentives for users to perform certain actions and, at the same time, may represent the currency of the system for acquiring certain services, such as the possibility to advertise. The Facebook of the future, thanks to technologies being rolled out today and subject to florid experimentation, will allow for decentralised ownership and distribution of the value created over time.

This is in stark contrast to the current version of Facebook. The company's name change to Meta was in part down to their bad press around privacy. Web 1.0 was all about converting analogue to digital in terms of information and systems. It was largely an information storage, search and exchange system. Web 2.0 was then all about sharing, whether information or resources. And Web 2.0 brought with it a weaponisation of advertising.

If it wasn't for the Cambridge Analytica scandal in 2018 and subsequent revelations, most consumers would still not be aware of just how much information was being gathered about them via social media and other platforms, which was then sold to advertisers. Algorithms could effectively profile a user based on their social media interaction, what they liked and commented on and even whether they slowed down their scroll to look at something in the feed. Those data points not only determined what that user saw on their feed, but it was pure gold for advertisers to sell more products. Worse still, it was used by bad actors to change what people believed in, what they believed was true and who they voted for. Users came to realise that centralised platforms such as Google and

Facebook knew a staggering amount of information on their users. The author of *Sapiens* and *Homo Deus*, Yuval Noah Harari, famously said, 'I didn't realise I was gay until I was 21, but Google probably knew at about 12[*].' Christopher Wiley, one of the Cambridge Analytica whistle-blowers, described what was being done unwittingly to consumers as 'psychological warfare' – using analytics to tap into a person's mood or sentiment and influence their 'hearts and minds' toward a particular outcome or candidate[†].

But it's not just the bad actors and the explosion of a post-truth world that people find upsetting. They are also tired of being thought of as a constant advertising target. It can be infuriating to look for a flight to Barcelona and suddenly be bombarded with flights, hotel options, excursion ideas and restaurants to visit in Barcelona – on every device we own. It's like we are being constantly digitally stalked and people are sick of it. The call for change was so loud that Apple issued an operating system update (iOS14.5) in 2021 which asked users to explicitly opt-in to allow companies to collect their data. Of course, millions chose not to and opted-out instead. The update cost Facebook a quarter of its annual profit[‡]. Google has indicated it will follow suit on Android but it's still not happened.

In Web 2.0 there was a saying: 'If the service is free, you are the product.' Tokens could change all that because instead

---

[*] Making Sense conversation between Sam Harris and Yuval Noah Harari (2020).

[†] Cadwalladr, C., 'The great British Brexit robbery: how our democracy was hijacked', *Guardian* (2017).

[‡] Naughton, J., 'For the first time in its history, Facebook is in decline. Has the tech giant begun to crumble?', *Guardian* (2022).

of being the product we become an invested enthusiast and user who can choose to give advertisers permission to access certain parts of our data in exchange for payment. Every time an API accesses our data, we get paid some sort of royalty. Those payments will be tokens, but it will then be possible to spend or swap those tokens on decentralised exchanges.

But the opportunities for change do not end there. Tokens may be used to influence the most important decisions of the network. Grasping this concept requires a mental leap of faith as we have been used to centuries of businesses owned by a single person or a small group. In the future, tokens will allow the entire community that uses a service to decide the direction to take. In the Facebook example, users, through their tokens, may be asked to vote on the possibility to accept the contentious matter of political advertising on the platform. This level of empowerment and shared governance will likely create stronger and more engaged communities where the communication between promoters and stakeholders is more frequent and alignment is increased.

> In the future, tokens will allow the entire community
> that uses a service to decide the direction to take.

Decentralised Autonomous Organisations (DAOs)

Earlier, when discussing NFT, we mentioned that Assange-DAO bought the *Clock* NFT. DAOs (pronounced *dowz*) are already changing the way people come together to achieve outcomes. In the NFT example, people came together to buy an NFT presumably because they support Julian Assange's cause and wanted to help him find a way to pay for his significant legal costs. But the people involved will never meet and probably don't know each other. In fact, there are over 10,000 people in the AssangeDAO.

Everything is agreed in the smart contract and executed without any intermediaries but most importantly without the need for trusting any of the other participants. Everyone who wanted to support the NFT purchase would have invested whatever they wanted in crypto and their investment would have been locked in a smart contract on the blockchain. If at the time of sale another buyer came in and bought the NFT, outbidding AssangeDAO, then the money would have been released back to the investors. If the bid was successful, the money would have been used for the execution of the purchase of the NFT, which would have been recorded on the blockchain.

We saw something similar in November 2021 when Sotheby's announced that it was going to auction off a rare copy of the US Constitution, one of only thirteen in existence. A group of people interested in purchasing the Constitution created a DAO called ConstitutionDAO and invited others to join. Within forty-eight hours, the DAO had raised $5 million, going on to raise a total of $34,025,859 in a matter of weeks*. This is an astonishing achievement for a group of people whose only connection was a desire to secure a rare asset. And it gives us a glimpse of the decentralised world to come.

For the most part, the sale of any significant asset from real estate to artwork to rare copies of the US Constitution would take weeks, even months to agree. The deal would have been hammered out by expensive lawyers and financiers

---

* https://juicebox.money/#/p/constitutiondao

behind a giant oak door, eventually signed to great fanfare on a stunning walnut table. The buyer would be paying for the corporate luxury and high salaries and both would be factored into the price. But with blockchain, smart contracts and tokenisation, new entities can be created overnight and decisions can be made in a simple, fair and transparent fashion. All the agreements and rules are coded into the smart contract and participation is open to everyone.

Although ConstitutionDAO failed to acquire the Constitution, it is another reminder of what is coming. The DAO also hints at how funds will be raised and businesses created in the future, where participants will also be part-owners via tokens.

Today public companies are run through boards of directors; in the future they may end up being governed by a DAO. Rules – articles of association and shareholder agreements – will all take new shapes and will be coded into a smart contract on a flexible blockchain like Ethereum or Solana. In a DAO, there is no hierarchy like there is in a typical business. Instead, ownership and governance rights are recorded on the blockchain and stakeholders may meet or interact on Discord, a communication platform popular in the crypto community. Votes will be cast and weighted according to the number of tokens held by all the stakeholders. Such stakeholders may acquire those tokens by showing a meaningful contribution to the organisation. The more tokens someone has, the more voting rights they have. This architecture is still not perfect, as evidenced by the Ethereum Name Service (ENS) DAO. Director of Operations for ENS, Brantly Millegan, shared some controversial personal opinions on Twitter and the rest of the DAO community was not impressed. A month-long debate followed about his suitability for the role. It was put to a vote but because the vote was based on one vote per token and not one vote per person, Millegan, who owned a lot of tokens, was able to narrowly keep his position. This can lead to stalemate governance situations, but these issues will be ironed out in time.

Today public companies are run through boards of directors; in the future they may end up being governed by a DAO.

Decentralised Finance (De-Fi) and the Digital Future

Everything we have described in this chapter so far is essentially coming together to facilitate a revolution in finance with a shift from centralised finance (Ce-Fi) to decentralised finance (De-Fi).

De-Fi is essentially a category of financial services and applications that operate on a decentralised, blockchain-based infrastructure. Its key aim is to recreate and innovate traditional financial systems by leveraging many of the building blocks we've discussed in Chapter 4 and earlier. In other words, big data, AI, process automation and the growth of powerful networks on the blockchain together with cryptocurrencies, tokens and tokenisation are removing the need for trusted third parties or intermediaries such as banks, financial services companies or other centralised entities. Blockchain and smart contracts allow the trust to be coded into the transaction.

Everything is coming together to facilitate a revolution in finance with a shift from centralised finance (Ce-Fi) to decentralised finance (De-Fi).

De-Fi is challenging the centralised financial system by empowering individuals with peer-to-peer transactions through a vast network utilising security protocols, connectivity, software and hardware advancements. In the centralised model, intermediaries rightly charge for using their service but De-Fi uses blockchain and DLT technology to reduce the need for those third parties and their associated costs. It is the network per se that provides the service, with a significant cost reduction.

As Rafal Cosmon, CEO and co-founder of TrustToken, points out, *Decentralized finance is an unbundling of traditional finance. [It] takes the key elements of the work done by banks, exchanges, and insurers today—like lending, borrowing, and trading—and puts it in the hands of regular people*.

The convergence between financial technology, decentralised networks and the exponential growth of artificial intelligence is shaping what we call the 'digital future' and redefining the financial services sector. Not only is this more efficient, faster and less expensive, it is helping to create a more resilient financial system too (Figure 5.2).

In a centralised system, as mentioned earlier, the whole system is vulnerable because there is, by definition, a single point of failure. A single point of failure (SPOF) refers to a component or part of a system that, if it fails, will cause the entire system to malfunction or cease functioning. In other words, it is a critical point in a system where the failure of that point can lead to the failure of the entire system.

---

* Napoletano, E. and Adams, M., 'What Is DeFi? Understanding Decentralized Finance', *Forbes* (2023).

Web3

Web3 empowers a more resilient, permissionless and decentralised collective ownership model

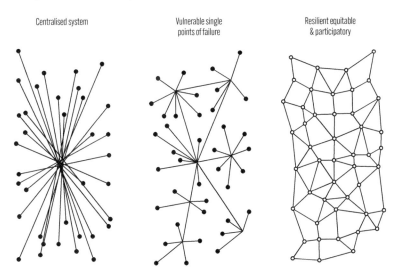

Centralised system   Vulnerable single   Resilient equitable
     points of failure   & participatory

Figure 5.2: The Differences Between Centralised
Systems and Decentralised Systems

The concept is often used in the context of designing and analysing the reliability and resilience of systems, including technological, organisational, infrastructural and financial systems.

This idea ties into Complexity Theory, around complex dynamic adaptive systems that encompass both fintech and blockchain. It is this idea of a SPOF that relates to a system's robustness, adaptability and resilience. Complexity Theory studies complex systems and their behaviour, emphasising the interactions among components and the emergence of patterns and behaviours that are not easily predictable from the properties of individual parts.

For example, Complexity Theory highlights the inter-connected nature of systems, where the behaviour of the whole emerges from the interactions of its components. In a centralised system with a single point of failure, this interconnectedness can be disrupted, creating negative cascading effects on the entire system. But in a decentralised system that weakness is prevented.

Complex systems also exhibit resilience and adaptability. If there is a disturbance, the system will continue to function, while adaptability is the capacity to adjust and evolve in response to changes. Identifying and addressing single points of failure is crucial for maintaining the resilience and adaptability of complex systems. This is why De-Fi will always be superior to Ce-Fi in terms of robustness.

In addition, Complexity Theory recognises that the relationship between cause and effect in complex systems is often non-linear. This means that a small change or failure in one part of the system can lead to disproportionately large and unpredictable consequences. A single point of failure exemplifies this non-linear behaviour as the failure of a seemingly minor component can have significant reper-cussions, as evidenced by the GFC. Again, De-Fi eliminates this danger, or at least significantly reduces it.

Redundancy and diversity in a system can also enhance its stability. Redundancy involves having back-up or alternative components that can take over in case of a failure. This redundancy and diversity is built into De-Fi by the nature of the decentralised network, whereas it is often limited in Ce-Fi because of budget constraints.

And, finally, complex systems are often adaptive, capable of self-organisation and self-adjustment. Again, because there is no longer a single point of failure in De-Fi, the system itself adapts allowing it to evolve and respond to changing conditions.

Blockchains are a form of complex adaptive dynamic systems, and they are the cornerstone of De-Fi networks. It is an expression of Complexity Theory where each part of the system adapts in response to changes in its environment, making it resilient to shocks. This resilience is a crucial factor in the construction of financial services infrastructure. These and other Web 3.0 technologies extend this idea further by enabling decentralised applications (DApps) and decentralised autonomous organisations (DAOs), paving the way for a future where financial transactions are more transparent, secure and devoid of central control.

Fintech, at its core, is revolutionising traditional financial services from mobile banking to automated investment advisors. But it is not just enhancing existing services, it is creating new paradigms for economic exchange. In platform economies, fintech serves as the backbone, providing efficient, user-friendly and accessible financial services. It has democratised access to financial tools, allowing even the most remote users to participate in the global economy.

In platform economies, fintech serves as the backbone, providing efficient, user-friendly and accessible financial services.

And of course, AI is a significant catalyst in this evolving landscape. Its role in processing vast amounts of data, predicting market trends and personalising financial services is indispensable. AI algorithms are becoming increasingly sophisticated, enabling them to handle complex financial tasks with greater accuracy and efficiency. The integration of AI in fintech and blockchain-based platforms is not just accelerating the growth of financial services but also ensuring they are more adaptive and responsive to consumer needs.

But it is important to appreciate that this intersection of fintech, Web 3.0 and AI is not just a confluence of technologies; it represents a unified economic element that is greater than the sum of its parts. This integration is leading to the creation of more robust, efficient and inclusive financial systems. It's a digital future where financial services are more accessible, transactions are more transparent and economic opportunities are more widely distributed.

In this digital future, the focus is not just on the technological aspects but also on how these technologies can be leveraged to create a more equitable and sustainable economic system. De-Fi offers a way to reduce systemic risks and provide a more stable financial environment. At the same time, AI's predictive capabilities can be used to identify and mitigate potential economic crises.

Digital Assets in the Real World

Let's revisit Libby and James one more time to explore how digital assets will not only change the nature of business but change wealth creation opportunities in the future for small and medium businesses.

When Libby ran Owen's there were no real digital assets beyond some professional photography that was used online to promote products or digital copies of the Owen's business livery to be used in promotional material.

But the world is very different by the time James takes over. James expands Libby's vision of a fully functional ecommerce business and moves out into a broader product range than just shoes. James was fascinated when Nike released the Nike Cryptokicks and Adidas sold NFTs. If other shoe businesses were making money in the digital space, why couldn't he?

As he grew up in the shoe-selling business, James became a sneaker collector in his teens and had been adding to his collection over the years. Much like comics or trading cards, pristine limited-edition trainers still in their box had become a well-established collectors' market. A pair of Air Jordan 11 'Jeter' would have cost you $400 in 2017 when they were released and yet a pristine pair still in the box are now worth anywhere between $30,000–$50,000[*]. They don't even need to be in pristine condition. A pair of Nike Air Yeezy Sample shoes worn by Kanye West at the 2008 Grammy Awards, sold for $1,800,000[†].

James was hooked and an idea began to take shape. Instead of it being a hobby, could he incorporate his passion into the business? Just for fun, he starts designing digital shoes for avatars in various metaverse projects such as Horizon Worlds, The Sandbox, Decentraland and Roblox. In many of these digital worlds, creators like James can sell accessories for users to dress their character or avatar within the world. James's designs were eye-catching and innovative. They appealed to the gamer audience first but his designs soon gained traction and he found a loyal fan base for his unique style shoes. James opened a Discord channel, where he chats with fans about existing designs and gets new ideas and input about new designs, while also ensuring more sales when the digital trainer is then launched. The fans feel part of the journey and James loves the interaction and creative process.

---

[*] No Author, 'High Kicks Meet High Fashion: The Most Expensive Sneakers of All Time', Luxe Digital (2023).

[†] Tapia, A., 'The 10 Most Expensive Sneakers Ever Sold', *Newsweek* (2021).

The success of these digital trainers makes him wonder if he could take them into the real world too. Of course, designing and launching a digital trainer is significantly cheaper than making the real thing that someone buys to put on their non-digital feet. The business is doing well but it's too much of a risk to invest too much of Owen's's working capital into the shoe manufacturing process. But James is tech savvy and he finds an ingenious solution. He designs a series of shoes and shows them to his Discord fans. The fans give him an idea of the potential appeal of certain designs in the real world by buying the associated NFTs. The price of the NFTs ends up funding the order for the shoe manufacturer and fans will be able to claim their shoes thanks to the NFT. How can James convince fans to put up the capital for shoes that they will not receive for months? How can they trust him? The answer is easy: they do not need to trust him. James creates two smart contracts.

The first one is signed with the fans who want to buy the trainers. It stipulates that fans will obtain an NFT that gives them access to a pair of sneakers in the new collection in exchange for ETH. Those ETH are not transferred to James's wallet but they are locked in the smart contract. They will be released to James only after an oracle (in this case the courier) confirms that the shoes have been delivered to the NFT holder.

The second smart contract is with the supplier in China. Normally the supplier would require full payment upfront before starting production. The smart contract allows James to pay only 30 per cent upfront; the rest of the payment is made on delivery and guaranteed by the first smart contract. As soon as the courier confirms delivery of the shoes, the first contract pays ETH from the fan to James and the second contract simultaneously sends part of the ETH to the Chinese manufacturer. The amount of ETH transferred to the manufacturer includes a small portion of the profits made by James to compensate for the delay in payment.

This is like what his mum did with schools in the local area, only now the agreements are made in smart contracts with people James has never even met. Everybody is aligned in a trustless system. If James does not order the shoes, these can't obviously be delivered and the ETH is returned to the client. If the shoes are produced, shipped and delivered, then the ETH is transferred and the manufacturer gets paid. James has effectively figured out a way to launch a new revenue stream for the business with a very limited amount of money in a way that was unimaginable when his mum was running the business.

Much to James's surprise, his real-world shoe design business grows and, within a few years, overtakes sales in the whole shoe division of Owen's's ecommerce business. James upgrades the existing ecommerce platform to a Web 3.0-enabled ecommerce website where fans can buy sneakers with cryptocurrency. This is a new paradigm for ecommerce that removes the risk of fraud and provides protection for consumers: money is transferred from the client wallet to the ecommerce wallet only after delivery is confirmed by the oracle. Consumers feel more protected. At the same time a Web 3.0 ecommerce website gets paid faster and with lower costs than they would with traditional credit card transactions. Another win/win. Best of all, James can grow the business without the need to reach out to banks, while the manufacturer can get access to the higher margins of retail sales. And the fans love it too because they are getting unique access to each new design series. The raving fans are especially excited when James's sneakers reach icon status and become a collectors' item.

Because so much of James's traditional business is operating through efficient fintech solutions, he can pass a lot of the day-to-day running of the business on to his senior managers, giving him more time to focus on his shoe designs. This is his passion.

All the sneakers are in limited-edition series and James has built up a loyal following with each new design having a long wait list. James wants to take advantage of this rarity effect. He partners with a famous singer. The singer, also very savvy when it comes to leveraging the opportunities offered by blockchain and Web 3.0, has her own utility token. This token is minted and assigned to fans as a reward for their engagement with the singer and her music on social media. When you watch a video on YouTube or include one of her songs in a playlist on Spotify, you receive tokens. Fans love it, because these tokens offer exclusive utility and reward them for doing something they would do anyway (listen to her music). They give fans access to exclusive merchandise collections, early access to ticket sales for concerts and special VIP passes. The singer is always looking for new ways to improve the utility of the tokens. James's shoes have reached iconic status and are incredibly rare. In partnering with James, the singer sees an opportunity to offer her fans exclusive access to the next limited-edition series. Through the partnership, all the singer's fans that own more than 100 tokens can stake them in exchange for an NFT that allows them to skip the waitlist and be the first ones to get the sneakers.

The digital asset future will open the door to tremendous opportunities, limited only by the creativity of tech-savvy entrepreneurs. As we have seen, James will not just be able to launch a new business line with a more limited amount of initial capital but he will also be able to sustain its growth by sharing the profits with third parties in a trustless fashion and will have the opportunity to reach a new group of customers and fans by collaborating with other entrepreneurs.

Chapter 6:
Opportunities and Challenges for the Future

There is little doubt that fintech presents a significant opportunity not only for investors but for underbanked consumers and business owners who are going to be able to plug into an ever-growing suite of products and services tailored to their needs. Instead of expensive one-size-fits-all services, these new fintech capabilities accelerated by tech innovation and AI will transform the financial services sector. Several trends will help accelerate this process.

AI

AI is a key capability that is set to open even more possibilities for fintech. One of the main advantages of fintech is that it allows companies to provide a product or service at a smaller scale. Instead of needing hundreds of thousands or millions of customers to be profitable, AI is allowing specialist fintech solutions to break even far faster and with significantly fewer customers, thus allowing for a wider array of niche products and services delivered via automation. Over time, we envisage an even greater impact of AI around:

- Origination
- Risk Underwriting and
- Customer Services

Origination

One of the most labour-intensive aspects of any business is lead generation and sales. We may have new ways to contact prospects and each innovation has created a new method of communication but sales has always been largely a human interaction – especially for B2B sales or large ticket items. Often these new methods have not been very effective, or they are effective to start with when the novelty of the new medium garners attention but their effectiveness diminishes over time. Most of us, for example, have received a spam email where our name has been spelled wrong or the sender is assuming an interest in a certain product or service based on information scraped from a website or bought from some list.

AI improvements are set to add a level of sophistication to this process that has been woefully missing in the past. For example, AI, together with big data and machine learning, will make time-consuming prospecting faster, easier and more productive, using a language that will appear more and more human.

> AI, together with big data and machine learning will make time-consuming prospecting faster, easier and more productive.

Most organisations already have a lot of data regarding customer behaviour and purchasing patterns, although they may not use it or know how to use it. AI will be able to identify these patterns and predict when clients are most likely to buy again or apply the intelligence to the rest of the sales pipeline to find others who fit that description. AI can therefore identify leads faster and sales teams don't therefore waste time chasing leads that are never going to convert. AI will also develop complex interactions with potential leads and there will be a point in the future in which AI will negotiate and close transactions based on data and experience of previous deals.

There are already platforms or capabilities that score prospects and qualify leads using AI and machine learning to identify the highest quality leads in a pipeline based on thousands of data points to give each contact a 'likelihood to close' score and allocate a contact priority to each record.

Part of the challenge in sales is knowing who to call in a limited time. Prior to these innovations, this often came down to who the salesperson wants to call or gut instinct. These types of AI and machine learning tools together with predictive AI will improve the process by ensuring time is maximised by calling on the people most likely to buy and not wasting time on those who are not.

AI in the future is likely to be so good that the initial contact and communication between the prospect and the salesperson will be automatically generated but personalised based on data collected from historical information about the prospect, any previous salesperson interaction with the prospect or their social media posts on platforms like LinkedIn. In effect, at some point in the future, all the contacts up to the point of meeting in person will be done by a machine and the person on the other end of the communication will be none the wiser. All the early communication, including personalised, AI-generated content is therefore taken care of automatically and, once the lead is qualified, a salesperson will step in to take over. Anyone who has used ChatGPT will know that it is already possible for AI to generate content that is indistinguishable from that created by a human being and this will only get more sophisticated over time.

AI will also be able to make predictions about what solutions would be most effective for the prospect and who in the organisation might be the best fit to close the sale. We think that human beings are unique, but when we have access to a lot of data it is possible to predict what is most likely to happen and act accordingly – all with very high degrees of accuracy. Not only does this represent a significant cost saving that will make access to products and services cheaper over time but it also represents a significant time saving which will allow salespeople to be much more effective.

Of course, the danger for a business using this technology when it is not yet perfect is a potential lack of trust. If prospects can tell that they are interacting with AI it can be off-putting, but it's likely our opinions about this will also change over time.

If we consider that 90 per cent of the business origination process today in financial services is manual, it is easy to deduct how meaningful the impact will be over the next decade, thanks to the evolution of AI. The drastic reduction in costs will have the double benefit of allowing businesses to service currently unbanked customers and to offer more tailor-made products to smaller client groups.

Risk Underwriting

Risk underwriting is also going to experience seismic change as AI improves and more data is collected and processed.

AI has already made a significant impact on risk under-writing in the financial and insurance industries and that impact will only increase as the technology improves and becomes more sophisticated. Those improvements will lead to:

- **Improved Data Analysis:** AI systems can process and analyse vast amounts of data from diverse sources more efficiently than traditional methods. This includes structured data such as credit scores and financial statements and unstructured data like social media activity or online behaviour. These bigger, more diverse datasets will provide a more comprehensive view of an individual or business's risk profile.
- **Enhanced Predictive Analytics:** Machine learning algorithms can already identify patterns and correlations in historical data to make more accurate predictions about future risks. This can help underwriters assess the likelihood of default, fraud or other risks with greater precision.
- **Real-time Monitoring:** AI allows for continuous monitoring of data in real time. This enables quicker identification of emerging risks or changes in a customer's financial situation, allowing underwriters to adjust risk assessments and take precautionary actions.
- **Automation of Routine Tasks:** AI can automate routine underwriting tasks, freeing up underwriters to focus on more complex assessments and decision-making. This will improve efficiency, reduce human error and streamline the underwriting process still further.
- **Behavioural Analysis:** AI algorithms can analyse behavioural data to understand individual and business behaviours, helping to identify patterns indicative

of potential risks. This can be especially valuable in detecting anomalies or changes in behaviour that may signal increased risk.

- **Integration of Alternative Data:** AI systems can efficiently identify and integrate alternative data sources that may not be traditionally considered in risk assessment. This could include data from social media, online reviews or, as mentioned in Chapter 4, the speed at which someone inputs data or how often they use the delete button in an application form. These types of non-traditional indicators will all come together to offer insights into an individual's or business's creditworthiness.
- **Customised Risk Models:** AI allows for the development of more personalised and dynamically adjusted risk models. These models can adapt to changing economic conditions, industry trends and individual circumstances, providing a more accurate reflection of current risk factors.
- **Improved Fraud Detection:** AI-powered systems can enhance fraud detection capabilities by identifying unusual patterns or inconsistencies in data, helping underwriters distinguish legitimate applications from potentially fraudulent ones.
- **Explainable AI:** As AI algorithms become more sophisticated, efforts are being made to ensure they are explainable and interpretable. This is crucial in the context of risk underwriting, where regulatory compliance and transparency are essential.

The use of AI in risk underwriting is a relatively consolidated part of the AI market. The real innovation in the future is unlikely to come from novel ways of analysing data but rather the ability to incorporate an increasing set of data points and train systems to clean the data to the maximum extent possible. Datasets are often full of mistakes or there are missing fields. Cleaning data is often considered the biggest challenge in data analysis. Even more than finding a good model to extract insights from it. It follows therefore that the results are always going to improve the cleaner the data becomes.

In addition, AI will help address another critical problem in risk underwriting: usually data science and risk management are different activities performed by different teams, with different skill sets. Whoever knows what constitutes a source of risk rarely knows how to handle data to gather insights and vice versa. The result is that ultimately companies find suboptimal solutions because of this separation of skills. In the future, AI will make data analysis much more user-friendly than it is today, allowing risk managers to handle and leverage data to an extent that has never been possible to them without the help of other teams.

There is little doubt that these advancements offer numerous benefits, including cost savings for customers and more streamlined operations, but it's important to address challenges such as bias in AI models, data privacy concerns and the need for ongoing human oversight to ensure responsible and ethical use of AI in risk underwriting. Regulations and industry standards will also play a role in shaping the adoption and implementation of AI in this domain.

> AI will make data analysis much more user-friendly than it is today, allowing risk managers to handle and leverage data to an extent that has never been possible.

Customer Service

Most people are already familiar with AI in customer service scenarios with the use of chatbots or using Amazon's Alexa or Apple's Siri. Most of us have had the frustrating experience of interacting with a chatbot that doesn't appear to be very intelligent at all.

What we so often forget when it comes to artificial intelligence is that what we are talking about is not real intelligence but rather pattern recognition supported by massive datasets. In other words, the chatbot is not listening to you like a human being might listen, it is simply matching what you ask to a list of possible solutions that may be relevant based on the words you used in your question. But the customer service of the future, thanks to advancing AI, is likely to be very different.

For example, chatbots and virtual assistants in the future will have advanced capabilities, thanks to ongoing developments in AI, natural language processing and machine learning. Enhanced Natural Language Understanding (ENLU) will allow chatbots to comprehend and respond to user queries in a more contextually aware and nuanced way. Multimodal interaction, including the ability to process and generate text, images and even video could make chatbots more dynamic and interactive in conversations. Advanced chatbots may even be equipped with emotion recognition capabilities to better understand and respond to the emotional state of the user. This in turn could lead to more empathetic and personalised interactions. Designed with continuous learning capabilities, the chatbots of the future will allow them to adapt and improve their performance over time, potentially becoming proactive in offering assistance, rather than just responsive to specific queries. It's also very likely that they will collaborate with human beings but in a more seamless way than is currently possible. Most chatbots can be interrupted and the user can ask to speak to a human but in the future, analysis will monitor the interaction and will transfer the conversation between automated and human-assisted mode as needed. At the same time, we will all be much more familiar with chatbots and AI. We will learn to communicate and ask questions in the most effective way. Just as over the years human beings refined their ability to make online searches on Google, the same will happen with AI-powered customer service interactions.

> **Chatbots and virtual assistants in the future will have advanced capabilities, thanks to ongoing developments in AI, natural language processing and machine learning.**

Additional users of AI to improve customer service include:

- **Automated Ticketing and Routing:** AI can automate the process of ticket creation and routing in customer service systems. This ensures that customer queries are directed to the right department or agent, improving response times and issue resolution.
- **Predictive Analytics:** AI analyses customer data to predict future needs, behaviours and potential issues. This enables proactive customer service, where businesses can address concerns before they escalate and offer personalised recommendations based on individual preferences.
- **Personalised Customer Interactions:** AI helps in personalising customer interactions by analysing customer data,

preferences and behaviours. This personalisation can extend to marketing messages, product recommendations and the overall customer journey, creating a more tailored and satisfying experience.

- **Voice Recognition and Speech-to-Text:** Voice-enabled AI systems can understand and respond to spoken language. This technology is used in voice-activated virtual assistants and customer service phone systems, streamlining communication and making it more accessible.

- **Sentiment Analysis:** AI can analyse customer feedback, reviews and social media mentions to gauge sentiment. This helps businesses understand how customers feel about their products or services, allowing them to respond appropriately and make improvements if necessary.

- **Automated Email Responses:** AI-powered systems can analyse and respond to emails, handling routine queries and categorising messages for human agents. This speeds up response times and ensures that urgent matters are addressed promptly.

- **Visual Recognition:** Visual AI can be used to analyse images and videos shared by customers. This is beneficial for industries like ecommerce, where customers might share photos of products with issues. Visual recognition can help identify problems and facilitate quicker resolutions.

- **Self-Service Options:** AI can power self-service options, such as interactive FAQs, knowledge bases and tutorials. This empowers customers to find solutions to their problems independently, reducing the need for direct customer support.

- **Continuous Learning and Improvement:** AI systems can learn from each customer interaction, continuously improving their understanding and response capabilities. This adaptive learning allows for more accurate and efficient customer service over time.

The main gain will be in relationship management cost savings. These savings will naturally lead to a reduction in cost of the service (such as the interest rate applied by a lending business) all else being equal.

Consolidation

Another significant opportunity will come through an inevitable consolidation process. Every innovation moves from disruption to consolidation. We have seen this in everything from the car to the computer to AI. During the disruption phase, there is a lot of experimentation and capital flows freely and copiously to the 'hottest tech' on display.

Take AI as an example. Back in 2013, funding to companies using AI was $3 billion, with fewer than 1,000 deals. In 2021, AI funding peaked at $69 billion across more than 4,000 deals[*] (Figure 6.1).

And that's just AI.

According to a Bain & Company analysis, from 2010 through 2020, tech start-ups made up most of the venture funding across all deals by independent venture capital (VC) firms and corporate venture capitalists (Figure 6.2)[†].

---

[*] Teare, G., 'Special Series Launch: The Promises And Perils Of A Decade Of AI', Funding Crunchbase (2022).

[†] Schallehn, M. and Johnson, C., 'Why Venture Capitalists Are Doubling Down on Technology', Bain & Company (2021).

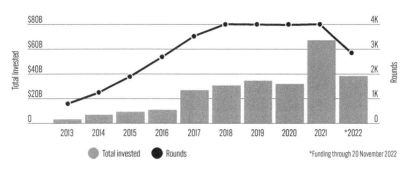

Figure 6.1: Annual Venture Investment in Companies Tied to AI

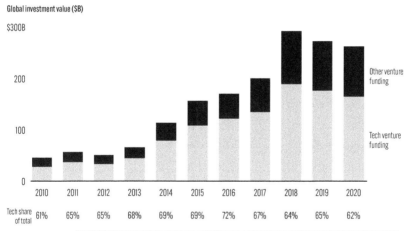

Figure 6.2: Tech Companies Consistently Receive
the Majority of Venture Funds

Needless to say, with so much money available during the last decade, VC firms were providing capital to a large number of competing businesses, and each one of them was hoping they were betting on the winning horse. But because of the tech frenzy, the level of scrutiny on the merit or validity of the idea or an analysis of how many similar businesses were backed by other investors were very superficial. Fear of missing out was the main driver of investments. It didn't really matter whether the idea was a good, bad or terrible one; if it involved tech, and especially AI, the money was received and the business was then in a dog-eat-dog fight with other similar businesses. Logic would say that the ones that survived were the best companies, but this was not always the case. A huge chunk of the money received by the start-up from the VC was not used to create the infrastructure or fine tune the business model; it was used in customer acquisition to quickly prove the concept and get to the next round of funding. We touched on this in Chapter 4 when discussing the challenges faced by the early P2P lenders, but the issue is also one experienced by fintechs more broadly. To survive they have no option but to pour vast sums of money into advertising to acquire customers. By some estimates, $0.40 of every $1 raised by start-ups from VCs end up in the pockets of Google, Facebook and Amazon[*]! As we said before, no wonder these companies have become trillion-dollar businesses over the last decade. Billions in venture capital are flowing into them as advertising revenue via start-ups desperate to acquire customers, prove concept and get the next tranche of funding to repeat the process.

> **By some estimates, $0.40 of every $1 raised by start-ups from VCs end up in the pockets of Google, Facebook and Amazon.**

---

[*] Seufert, E.B., 'Is it healthy for start-ups to spend so much money on user acquisition?', Mobile Dev Memo Content (2018).

However, capital is not always as available. 2022 marked a step change in the ability of start-ups and fintech companies to fundraise. Many of these companies are seeing their cash reserves collapsing and there is much more focus on efficiency and profitability. The consolidation process is kicking in and we are seeing more and more mergers and acquisitions, where previously competing businesses are talking to each other and joining forces to gain the economies of scale that will be needed to reach profitability. Most fintechs will need large balance sheets and strong origination to survive in the long term and too many are simply not big enough to survive.

As mentioned, part of the appeal and benefit of fintechs is that they can operate at a smaller scale compared to banks and traditional financial service businesses. Logic would say that this should negate the need for the type of consolidation that has occurred in the banking industry of the past decades. However, while the breakeven point of fintech companies may be significantly lower than that of traditional players, extreme competition by similar businesses trying to prove their model can lead to a lose/lose situation, certainly in the short term. Take, for example, a product such as revenue-based financing for ecommerce businesses. When it was launched, it was a novel idea with a good product market fit. This led to the proliferation of players in the market, with the natural consequence that pricing became extremely aggressive (to the point that it was not reflecting the underlying risk) and customer acquisition became tremendously expensive. This was one of the consequences of almost unlimited equity capital available to fintech start-ups during the 2020–2021 boom. The subsequent reduction in capital availability led to a sort of Darwinian 'survival of the fittest'. Consolidation, through merger and acquisition (M&A) or simply the failure of the least performing players will play a crucial role in shaping the future of finance.

> Consolidation, through merger and acquisition (M&A) or simply the failure of the least performing players will play a crucial role in shaping the future of finance.

Regulation

One of the biggest challenges facing fintech and whether all its promise is realised is regulation. For obvious reasons, it's very difficult and very expensive to become a fully licensed bank. In the UK, for example, the process involves establishing a legal entity for the bank, typically a public limited company (PLC) or a private limited company (Ltd). This includes meeting the Companies House requirements. Then the bank needs to meet the regulatory capital requirements set by the Prudential Regulation Authority (PRA). The capital requirements are designed to ensure the stability and solvency of financial institutions. The would-be bank must then submit a formal application to the Prudential Regulation Authority (PRA) and the Financial Conduct Authority (FCA). The application will include detailed information about the bank's business plan, financial strength, risk management processes, governance structure and compliance procedures. Key individuals involved in the management and governance of the bank, such as directors and senior executives, will undergo a 'fit and proper' assessment to ensure they have the necessary skills, experience and integrity. And the bank must show that it can implement robust internal systems and controls to ensure compliance with regulatory requirements, including anti-money laundering (AML) and Know Your Customer (KYC) procedures. The bank will also need to develop comprehensive risk management policies and procedures to identify, assess and manage various risks associated with banking activities while establishing a strong governance structure, including a board of directors and various committees to oversee the operations of the bank and ensure effective decision-making.

One of the biggest challenges facing fintech is regulation.

The regulatory authorities will then review the application, conduct due diligence and assess the bank's readiness. If satisfied, they will grant the necessary authorisations to operate as a fully licensed bank. Once authorised, the bank must continue to adhere to ongoing regulatory requirements and submit regular reports to the regulatory authorities.

There is a rationale behind such a strict and rigorous process. Because of reasons explained in the previous chapters, banking has always been a volume business. To be sustainable, banks must raise a large amount of capital through government-insured deposits and they must work closely with each other. The default of a bank, as experienced via the Lehman Brothers collapse during the GFC, is a very serious occurrence with grave consequences and tangible risk of repercussions throughout the system. Regulators can't afford to take such risks and so the fallout from the GFC led to rules and regulations becoming even more stringent.

It's therefore hardly surprising that not many new businesses apply to become a bank. Not only is it complex but the capital requirements and the time required to go through the process make it a next to impossible endeavour in most cases, especially for start-ups. And yet there is still a vast market of unbanked or underbanked consumers and SMEs that need what a bank is supposed to offer.

What is needed is a regulatory middle ground somewhere between a fully regulated company and a fully regulated bank so that fintech solutions can flourish. One of the biggest advantages that banks have is that they have access to deposits and those deposits are then used to generate profit for the bank. There are no deposits in venture capital-backed fintech start-ups. Right now, those start-ups might be paying a substantial interest rate to specialised institutional investors to get access to the money they need to offer their financial products. But if the regulators were to set up a more flexible regulatory system where fintechs could access deposits, at least to a certain extent, fintechs would be able to thrive and become profitable much faster than it is currently possible thanks to a reduced cost of funding.

Let's say, as an example, that different forms of banking licences, with different levels of maximum deposits and permissible activities, may be obtained with different applications and different requirements. Such a risk-based approach is currently unthinkable, as the memory of the GFC still lingers, but it could represent an extraordinary opportunity for the development of new financial services in the future.

> What is needed is a regulatory middle ground somewhere between a fully regulated company and a fully regulated bank.

This type of regulatory middle ground is only a matter of time, especially as the commercial banks have willingly retreated from certain sections of the market that they do not want to serve. One of those areas is SME lending and yet SMEs are the backbone of every economy. There will be growing pressure on regulators to recognise this disconnect and allow for middle-ground regulatory solutions to flourish.

Funding

Another significant challenge for fintech start-ups is funding. Unlike traditional start-ups, fintech start-ups, especially those offering lending products, need to raise both equity and debt to fund the loans issued to their customers. At the beginning, the industry thought of an ingenious way to solve this problem: peer-to-peer lending (P2P). The early fintech lenders acted as intermediaries between investors and borrowers, without the need for their own capital to be deployed. The company would originate loans and present them on a platform for funding. Investors could co-invest in the loan, earning a return generally higher than what was available to them in traditional investment products. In theory, this was a win/win scenario. However, as mentioned in Chapter 4, the P2P model suffered from two major problems:

- **Cost of acquisition:** Traditionally, lenders had to sustain costs to find borrowers and originate loans. In P2P, this issue is exacerbated. Not only do lenders need to market their lending product to borrowers, but they also need to find and maintain a robust base of investors, to make sure that each loan is funded in a reasonable amount of time once it is presented on the platform. This doubling of acquisition costs turned out to be an unsurmountable challenge for many of the P2P players.

- **Marketplace liquidity:** The availability of funds to issue loans is variable and unpredictable, especially when investors are retail and do not have any commitment to fund. This typically leads to liquidity problems, notably during a crisis, when the capital is most needed. The early Covid days, as an example, showed the weakness of the model and caused significant disruption across the industry.

Funding models developed substantially over the past few years and nowadays fintech companies have various ways to fund their loan books. Alternative credit providers emerged as a more credible and predictable source of funding and the interest rates charged were competitive with the P2P model. However, to reach institutional level cost of funding requires loan books to be above certain minimum thresholds and for the product to be 'bankable' (able to be lent against by large financial institutions). This obviously represents a challenge, as fintech start-ups end up being in a limbo with inefficient cost of funding until they reach a critical mass. Progress is being made in this space, with an increasing appetite by professional investors for these new alternative credit opportunities, but clearly the limited ability to access deposits does not help to address the cost of funding issue.

> Progress is being made in this space, with an increasing appetite by professional investors for these new alternative credit opportunities.

Equity Financing

The first ten to fifteen years of equity financing for early-stage fintech companies showed us the challenges of applying the traditional venture capital model to the new breed of financial services businesses. Mark Zuckerberg's famous motto, 'move fast and break things,' may well apply to the vast majority of early-stage companies. The primary objective of a start-up is not rolling out the perfect product, but rather to gather data and information that can lead to a rapid iteration of the product and constant improvement to the point where the so-called 'product-market fit' is finally reached. Time is of the essence, because the equity financing needed to sustain operating costs is a scarce resource. Hence, also VCs support the view that start-ups need to move fast, even if that means failing to reach the objective. An early failure saves money for future funding rounds in other, more successful projects.

This financing model worked well for the traditional VC-backed world, but it does not apply as well when going to market with a prototype is not an option. Biotech, for example, is definitely not one of those sectors where you want to move fast and break things. Making a mistake in biotech could risk human lives. That's the reason why, historically, funding for biotech companies has come from niche funds specialising in the sector. These funds understand that launching a successful biotech product is an endeavour that requires huge amounts of funding and a significantly longer time horizon than a traditional start-up to be deemed 'successful'.

Fintech does not risk human lives but handles money: savings, investments, loans, etc. The consequence of an early failure of a company handling retail investments could have very negative ramifications when compared to the failure of a social network or a gaming app. At the same time, a fintech lender with a sizeable loan book could cause significant damage in the industry if the quality of the risk underwriting was very weak right from the beginning. There is still only a partial understanding in the market of the peculiarities of fintech financing and still too many equity funders that underestimate the time horizon and the economic resources required to build a credible and sustainable player. This represents yet another challenge for the market that only time and experience will be able to tackle.

Considering the environment that these innovations are advancing in, the pace of technological development and the growing need from a market left behind by traditional banks, there is little doubt that fintech will flourish over the longer term inside a vast platform economy. The only question is when. We believe the opportunities still outweigh the challenges and those challenges will be surmounted.

Conclusion:
Redefining Financial Stability

In the ever-evolving landscape of financial services, the concept of 'narrow banking' can make a comeback as a beacon of stability and efficiency, in turn benefiting the model of non-bank lenders and fintech lending platforms across the globe.

> 'Narrow banking' can make a comeback as a
> beacon of stability and efficiency.

At its core, narrow banking is a financial model where banks restrict their activities primarily to accepting deposits and investing in secure, low-risk assets. Unlike commercial banks, which engage in a wide range of financial activities including riskier asset investments, complex derivative trading and several turns of leverage, narrow banks, with their emphasis on low (virtually zero) leverage and full equity-backed credit exposure, focus on stability and reduced risk exposure. This model inherently shields them from the sort of systemic risks that have periodically rattled the global financial markets.

This approach sharply contrasts with the traditional operations of 'bulge bracket' banks and offers a promising avenue for sustainable lending to the real economy – particularly to small and medium-sized enterprises (SMEs) and consumers. 'Bulge bracket' refers to a group of leading and globally recognised investment banks that are traditionally involved in large and complex financial transactions. These banks typically have a significant presence in international financial markets and offer a wide range of financial services. The term 'bulge bracket' originally referred to the listing of banks on the upper rows or 'bulges' of the league tables that rank investment banks by deal volume. The problem is that these bulge bracket banks or major players are no longer offering a wide range of financial services and they are certainly not servicing a wide range of customers, leaving far too many consumers and SME operators unbanked or underbanked.

The rise of narrow banking is not just a theoretical adjustment but a practical response to the glaring traditional banking system vulnerabilities we have discussed in this book, accentuated by the Digital Revolution in financial services. What's different is that the concept of narrow banking has now expanded to include non-bank lenders to the real economy, including credit asset managers and fintech lending platforms. As such, fintech companies are the banking system's stabilisers.

Systemic Risks in Traditional Banking

The fragility of traditional banks was starkly highlighted by the 2023 crisis involving Silicon Valley Bank (SVB) and Credit Suisse. These cases demonstrated the acute risk of liquidity crises, where a rapid withdrawal of deposits, fuelled by a loss of confidence, can lead to a bank's collapse at an astonishing speed. This risk is magnified in the digital era, where large-scale fund transfers can be executed instantly and information as well as unfounded rumours can spread around the globe in a matter of seconds, amplifying the potential for significant bank runs. Panic may be instant but it can still create outsized and lasting damage. Unlike the bank runs of the past, today's digital banking environment can lead to a rapid erosion of a bank's deposit base, underlining the need for more stable banking models. What has really changed in the past few years is the velocity, and with velocity comes far greater danger of uncontrollable outcomes.

Panic may be instant but it can still create outsized and lasting damage.

In the past, a period of panic would be followed by bank runs, where depositors would queue up outside the bank branches distributed across the territory. But the bank would still close at night and over the weekend, giving time to implement remedial actions and construct a solution or simply give time for the truth to quash the rumour and the panic to die down. Today, no one is queuing outside branches, even if they could find one to queue outside. Instead, vast amounts of money on deposit can disappear with a swipe or a click on a mobile-only cloud-based app, leaving no time for remedial actions and allowing a moment of panic to explode like a deadly virus. This has vast ramifications for systemic risk at the aggregate level of the financial system. Most metrics utilised today, including liquidity coverage ratios (LCRs), are not fit for purpose. They don't allow for the proper assessment of modern banking liquidity and certainly don't indicate the risk of deposits disappearing overnight, referred to as the 'daily liquidity risk' or risk of 'flash runs'.

Credit Suisse, then the second largest bank in Switzerland, exemplifies the fragility of the system at times of turmoil and the deadly effect of the daily liquidity risk. A moment of panic and imbalance can create catastrophic consequences. Such is the very definition of complex and inherently fragile systems that can be tripped up by relatively minor shocks. The real question that should be posed is what would have happened if Credit Suisse's crisis had spread out to another large European bank and what would the safety net have looked like. Would the relatively small Swiss National Bank (SNB), Central Bank of Switzerland, have been able to stem the flow?

By the same token, it would seem imaginable and consequential for several financial institutions to be at risk of flash runs, and in time be just a few crises moments away from full consolidation into the respective Central Banks.

Shift in Lending Practices

In the United States, a notable shift has occurred with 80 per cent of total loans now being handled outside traditional commercial banks. This trend points to an increasing reliance on alternative lending platforms and asset managers, a shift not yet fully replicated in Europe. European banks, mired in their own challenges of fragmentation and inefficiency, continue to provide over 80 per cent of the corporate funding through bank loans – the opposite to the market structure visible in the US. However, a gradual transition is observable, as these institutions strive to catch up with their American counterparts and prepare for a more digitally oriented future in lending.

The European banking market is as fragmented as it is notoriously resistant to change. The issue is one of breadth of operations. Hardly a bank in Europe is a champion in more than one or two countries across the Continent. It is a result of the fatigue in creating a fully functional EU single market, a banking union across the EU, a complete EU capital markets union. Amongst the unpleasant consequences is a funding gap in the trillions of Euros for SMEs in the Continent. If banks are the only game in town, but are dysfunctional and unable to provide much-needed solutions, the system will rebalance itself in ways that make it more efficient, stable and sustainable. Enter . . . new technologies.

Technological Advancements Reshaping Banking

Technology in financial services has many faces, but two outlined thoroughly in this book are fintech platforms and blockchain. Fintech platforms have emerged in the last decade to reinvent the borrowers' experience in ways that make it more frictionless, more user-friendly, more cost-efficient and faster, while still laying over traditional banking rails. Within it, fintech lending advanced as a new force in town, in parallel to traditional bank lending. To some extent, fintech lending is the emerging property of a system in transition, the alternative path for the system to rebalance itself away from the inefficiencies and rigidities of centralised banking structures unwilling to adjust to the necessities of their clients within the digital age. It is the response of the fragile system itself while it seeks a new equilibrium or stable state.

Further out on the technological spectrum, blockchain and Web 3.0 reinvent financial rails altogether from the ground up in what looks like a second derivative of change beyond fintech platforms. Platforms are transformative but consequential and accretive; blockchain and the apps built on it are antagonistic, disruptive, cathartic. At current rates, the combination of the two seems inescapable, and likely to affect the shape of financial services for decades to come. They represent the veins and arteries of the new financial markets, while AI and computing power is the oxygen running through them.

> Fintech platforms and blockchain represent the veins and arteries of the new financial markets, while AI and computing power is the oxygen running through them.

Technology, particularly blockchain, is playing a transformative role in the financial sector. One of the most interesting use cases is the tokenisation of real-world assets (RWA), streamlining transactions and drastically reducing operational costs. The operational cost comparison between traditional banking giants and blockchain-based platforms (such as Uniswap) is staggering, reflecting billions in annual potential savings. These savings will be experiences from back office to middle office, from custodial services to clearing and settlement/trading, from IT to compliance costs.

This technological revolution is not only about efficiency; it also implies a more vibrant banking environment with reduced client retention, as customers can easily switch providers at the first sign of trouble. This adds to systemic risks; it fuels the 'daily liquidity risk' significantly. If bank runs cannot lose steam overnight or over the weekend, at such times when the bank is closed, what can stop even the slightest moments of idiosyncratic stress to a single large institution having knock-on effects into broader systemic issues?

And if the system has two parallel channels, one fragile and the other one resilient, where do we realistically expect the system to balance out over time? Evolution tells us that the fragile ecosystem will disappear in favour of the resilient system.

Intersection of Fintech, Web 3.0 and AI

The convergence of fintech platforms, blockchain/Web 3.0 and AI are creating a new wide-ranging economic ecosystem. This ecosystem when viewed as a whole, seems a very plausible future state for market economies. This intersection is consistent with the emerging theory of decentralised systems as inherently more resilient to shocks, a concept deeply embedded in the Complexity Theory of dynamic adaptive systems. In this context, fintech represents the evolution of financial services, blockchain the reinvention of financial infrastructure and AI the catalyst accelerating these transformative tectonic shifts. Add to this a funding model where capital is provided as pure equity and the set of characteristics of this new financial ecosystem makes it a superior solution to much of the fragility we are seeing today.

> The convergence of fintech platforms, blockchain/Web 3.0 and AI are creating a new wide-ranging economic ecosystem.

In conclusion, narrow banking and asset management emerge not just as alternative financial practices but as necessary adaptations to a rapidly changing economic landscape, running fast into the 'Digital Future' of financial services. They offer a sustainable solution to soften the blow from systemic risks while effectively serving the real economy. As we embrace a digital future, marked by the interplay of fintech, blockchain and AI, narrow banking stands as a testament to the potential for stability and efficiency in a world where traditional financial models no longer suffice. This paradigm shift is not merely a financial evolution; it is a necessary response to the complexities and vulnerabilities of our modern economic systems. It is hard to underestimate the bombshell opportunity in such transformational times, as the players of tomorrow will look very different from the players of today.

Index

INDEX

INDEX

Francesco:

To my beloved wife Jessica, whose steadfast support and inspiration makes me live, and to our brilliant boys, Leonardo, Gabriele and Davide, lights of my life. To the wider Fasanara family, whose fortitude and humour have unwittingly filled these pages, I extend my deepest gratitude. *Familia supra omnia* – family above all. This tome is a testament to our shared journey, adorned with laughter and love. May it serve as a beacon of the joy we've woven together in discovering and helping to shape an entirely new asset class.

Daniele:

To my precious wife, Federica, and cherished daughter, Beatrice. Your unwavering support has been the cornerstone of my journey towards realising my dreams. I am endlessly grateful for your encouragement and steadfast presence in my life.

To the dedicated members of the Fasanara team. Your bright insights, invaluable assistance and infectious smiles have made every step of this journey both meaningful and joyous. Together, we are more than colleagues – we are family.

And to those who inadvertently became my greatest teachers by placing obstacles in my path. Your challenges, though daunting at times, have only served to fortify my resolve and deepen my determination to achieve something meaningful in life.